THE BASIC GUIDE TO
Dyeing & Painting
FABRIC

CINDY WALTER & JENNIFER PRIESTLEY

Published by

kp krause
publications
since 1952

PO Box 5009 • Iola WI 54945-5009 • krausebooks.com

Please call or write for our free catalog of publications. Our toll-free number to place an order or obtain a free catalog is 800-258-0929 or please use our regular business telephone 715-445-2214 for editorial comment and further information.

Library of Congress Catalog Number 2001097823
ISBN 0-87349-334-6

Close-up of one quilt from Melody Johnson's Chamber Series. The series includes five works, completed in February 2000. For more information, see page 64.

Table of Contents

Close-up of Kitties for Theresa, page 17, by Cindy Walter.

Authors' Introduction

Cindy Walter

From Cindy

Colors have been the inspiration for many of my quilts. As a quilting book author and teacher I continually encourage students to freely experiment with their choices of color, because most quilts are simply about color and its density. In 1995, wanting to add more color to my quilts, I created the successful technique of Snippet Sensations, which uses bits of fabric to create multi-hued designs of fabric art. The technique was easy and provided an outlet for my artistic side. I was able to create a "painting" by "throwing" fabric quickly onto my fabric canvas.

It was only natural that I would evolve from using fabric as my "paint" to actually painting on my fabric. So, in the past few years I started to paint fabric. Before working with Jennifer, I was intimidated with dyeing and painting fabric and unfortunately started each piece in trepidation and with a specific goal in mind. That has all changed for the better.

While taking a painting workshop from Jennifer in her studio I learned that **fabric painting is fun**! Forget about setting goals. Learn to let go of your initial inhibitions and begin to freely paint without predetermined ideas about the results. The more relaxed you become, the more pleased you will be by the results. Remember, there is no such thing as an ugly piece of fabric; it just turned out differently than you expected.

Because I've admired Jennifer's uniquely painted fabric for years, imagine my delight when we became partners in writing this book. What we have tried to do is teach you the basics for transforming plain pieces of fabric into individual works of art. Painting and dyeing fabric is in its infancy, waiting for you to take it one step further, so **explore**.

Cindy Walter

Other books by Cindy Walter.

Snippet Sensations

More Snippet Sensations

Fine Hand Quilting

Attic Windows

Basic Appliqué

From Jennifer

Jennifer Priestley

From a very early age colors fascinated me—and they still do to this day. I've never been able to draw well, but I've never been afraid to experiment, and I've always been curious about color. I would frequently feel an urge to paint everything in sight and needed to surround myself with color.

I was introduced to quilting by a neighbor when she encouraged me to take a class. My first quilting teacher, Sue Stedman, remains an inspiration and created two of the quilts pictured in this book. After seeing a quilt constructed with hand-painted fabrics by Barbara Barber, I knew I wanted to use them in my quilts. So, I began painting my own fabrics.

It wasn't long after I started hand-painting fabric for my own projects that my friends wanted pieces for their projects. Eventually, I was painting fabric almost everyday. Thus, my hand-painted fabric company, Fabrics To Dye For, was born in 1995. Now I make my living painting thousands of yards of fabric each year. Painting fabric isn't work for me; I love every minute of this adventure. My fabric has been featured in numerous publications, and now I am designing commercial lines.

A heartfelt thanks to my wonderful husband, Joe, for all of his support, and for taking care of the kids while I'm working, and to our three fabulous children, Pammy, Joe, and Sam. Your artwork and love are a great inspiration. I love you all.

Jennifer W. Priestley

In Gratitude

Jennifer and Michael Katz, founder of Rupert, Gibbon & Spider, playing with dyes and paints in the Jacquard studio.

We thank our families and friends who supported us through the challenging, though rewarding, process of writing this book. We also thank Jennifer's mother, Jane P. Varcoe, who spent countless hours in her studio painting several of the fabrics pictured in this book, including the piece for the cover. We love you, Jane!

Thanks to all of the talented designers who created original projects for this book and to the professional dyers who shared their unique styles of dyeing and painting. We especially thank Joyce Mori and Cynthia Myerberg, authors of **Dye It! Paint It! Quilt It!**, for sharing their gradation formula.

A special thank you to the staff of Rupert, Gibbon & Spider, Inc., the makers of Jacquard dye and paint products, for their generous supply of technical knowledge and photographs.

Blooming 9-patch, 102" x 102", 2001, by Susan E. Stedman. This striking quilt comes from a pattern in the book Tradition with a Twist, *by Blanche and Darlene Young. Susan, a long-time quilting teacher, made this quilt for Jennifer with painted fabrics from Fabrics To Dye For. It was machine quilted by Marilyn Badger. In the private collection of Richard and Jane Varcoe.*

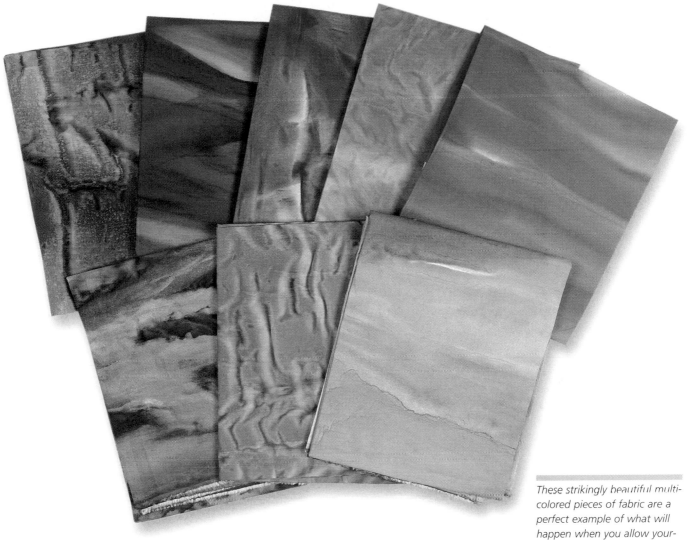

These strikingly beautiful multi-colored pieces of fabric are a perfect example of what will happen when you allow yourself creative freedom.

Introduction to Dyeing and Painting Fabric

The purpose of this book is to teach you that creating your own pieces of unique fabric is not only captivating, but it's also an extremely rewarding form of creative expression. You do not have to be an artist to paint or dye fabric. Relax, play, and don't start with a specific result in mind. Work with colors you like. Mix two or three small containers of paint or dye and then have fun.

Many books have been written on the topic of coloring fabric, all with their own recipes for success. We want you to know there is no right or wrong process as long as you are getting good results. Our goal is to provide you with a solid foundation for further experimentation.

Even though dyes and paints are two differ-

ent mediums, they can be used in similar ways; for example, you can paint with dyes by adding a thickener to liquid dye, or you can "dye" with paint by diluting it with water. But, for the most part, they have different characteristics and require different technical directions. Because of this, we have presented dyes and paints in two separate sections of this book.

Our goal is to "get you started" by introducing you to the common dyeing and painting methods used by fiber artists. Our instructions and "recipes" are just guidelines. Use your creativity to expand beyond what we have taught you. For more information on dyes, paints, and applications, we encourage you to read the books in the Recommended Reading section, page 94.

For your convenience, many of the products in this book are available in "kit" form. For more information write or email the authors, or visit www.FabricsToDyeFor.com.

Overview

The photo at right shows a variety of color dyed with the immersion technique, using all three primary colors. Jennifer easily created this grouping with a direct dye kit from G & K.

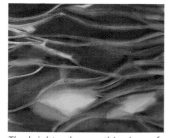

Jennifer painted this beautiful fabric, which has a calming effect.

The bright colors on this piece of fabric, painted by Jane Varcoe, are invigorating.

Color

Colors have personalities, just like people. For the most part, yellows are vivacious, oranges are warm, and reds are passionate and aggressive, while blues are cool and calm and purples are regal and theatrical. Greens can be as vibrant as yellow or as calm as blue because they are made from a combination of those colors. Color evokes emotions in people because of these characteristics. We suggest you start painting with colors you like. Then, to add a spark to your projects, we challenge you to use colors you do not like—you may surprise yourself!

Even though dyes and paints are manufactured and available in many colors, there will be times when you may not have the color available that you need. Or you might want to change the tone of a certain color, so you will need to blend colors. Study the color triangles on the next page so you understand how the different colors are created. All colors are created from a combination of one or more of the three primary colors and possibly with a touch of black or white for shading. You do not have to be an expert in color theory to use dyes or paints, nor do you have to remember the following information, but it is helpful when you want to mix colors to achieve more interesting hues.

Primary Colors

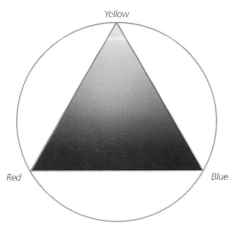

Secondary Colors

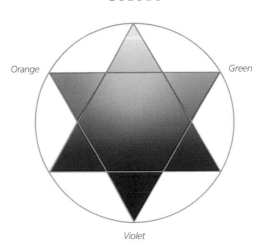

Intermediate Colors

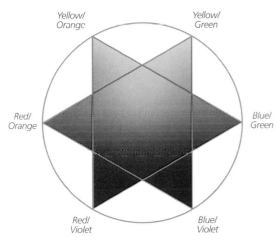

Complementary Colors

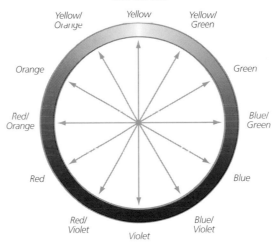

■ **Hue** is the word identifying a color by its name, i.e., blue, red, yellow, etc.

■ All colors, or hues, are derived from three **primary colors**: blue, red, and yellow. (**Note:** There are other color theories that use different primary colors, such as cyan, magenta, and yellow).

■ Mixing two primary hues creates **secondary colors**: red + yellow = orange; red + blue = purple; and yellow + blue = green.

■ Mixing a secondary color with additional amounts of one of the primary colors produces **intermediate** colors: blue + red (= purple) + blue = blue violet.

■ **Tertiary** colors, such as brown, contain a mixture of all three primary colors.

■ **Complementary** colors are those which are exactly opposite each other on the color wheel

■ The **shade** of a color can be changed by adding black or white. It can be tinted or dulled by adding gray.

■ The **value** of a color, its lightness or darkness, is controlled by adding black, white, or gray and by diluting dyes and paints with water.

Study the bands of the color triangle; use it to discover how you can mix and achieve the colors you desire. Further, experiment and learn to use primary, secondary, intermediate, tertiary, and complementary colors.

We painted this color wheel using Jacquard Silk Colors and the CMYK color theory, which uses cyan, magenta, yellow, and black (instead of the more common color theory, which uses blue, red, and yellow). The outer ring shows the primary colors and the secondary colors. The next rings are either lightened by diluting the dye with water or darkened by adding black dye. Finally, the center wedges are tertiary colors created by combining the complementary color from the opposite side of the wheel.

DYES
- Soluble
- Don't always reveal color instantly
- Fabric specific
- Set with chemical or steam
- Dye makes solutions
- No white
- Hand of fabric not affected
- Transparent

PAINTS/PIGMENTS
- Insoluble
- Show color right away
- Any fabric
- Must be heat set
- Pigment is in suspension
- Have white
- Hand of fabric affected
- Opaque or semi-transparent

Colorant

When the topic of colorants arises, the most frequently asked questions include, "What are the differences between paint and dye?"; "What is the difference in the end results?"; and "When should you use which product?"

The pigment colors in paint are particles that have to be glued (bonded) to the surface of the fabric in some fashion, whereas dye is a chemical colorant in a particle-less solution that binds itself into the fabric fibers. Because dyes are totally transparent, they allow the luster of the fabric to shine through the colors. Paints, even semi-transparent pigments, sit on top of the fabric fibers and, in some cases, mask the fabric's true luster. Dyes do not affect the hand, or feel, of fabric, whereas paints may make the fabric slightly stiffer. Paints are usually set with heat by ironing or placing the fabric in a clothes dryer. Dyes, depending on the type, are set with either heat (steam) or chemicals.

Everyone should experiment with both dyes and paints, because each has its own unique qualities. You may want to purely use paint, purely use dye, or a combination of the two. Just as if you were combining fabric textures on a garment or quilt, it is a matter of personal preference and experimentation. Look at the comparisons in the chart at left for more information.

Fabrics

Both fiber-reactive dyes and fabric paints work with all natural cellulose fibers, such as cotton, linen, viscose, rayon, and also silk (a protein fiber with cellulose "look-a-like" molecules). We use fiber-reactive dyes or fabric paints in the projects in this book, so we recommend you use these natural fabrics.

Mercerized cotton fabric is excellent for dyeing because it absorbs the dye, causing the colors to appear stronger. Jennifer prefers Pima cotton, because of its tight, fine weave. We've had great success with all types of silk; silk's luster shows with dyes, but it is somewhat masked with paint.

For predictable results when dyeing or painting, use a fabric that is prepared for dyeing (PFD). This means the fabric is washed free of resins, sizing agents, oils, and other materials used in the weaving or printing process. Avoid fabrics with any type of finish such as permanent press or stain-resistant. While PFD fabric is not always found in stores, it is available from the sources listed in the back of this book (page 94). You can also create your own by washing the fabric in Synthrapol, an economical, industrial-strength detergent used as a pre-wash and after-wash for fabric in the dyeing and painting process.

If you want to dye wool or polyester, you will need to use different types of dye (acid dyes for wool and disperse dyes for polyester) that we do not cover in this book. You can find supplies for these dyes in the sources section.

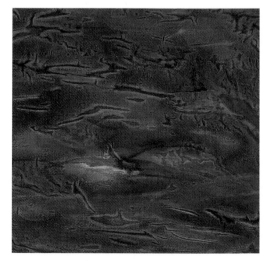

Areas on the same piece of fabric can turn out differently because of chemicals in the fabric, the dampness of the fabric, drying time, and the mixing of the dyes or paints.

Blocks, 25" x 42", 1996, by Jennifer Priestley. Do not be afraid to mix different types of fabrics in one project. This quilt is the rewarding result of experimentation. The entire project is made from hand-painted and -dyed silk, velvet, and cotton; commercial lamé and polyester sheer fabric were added as embellishment. Jennifer made this for her husband as a present for his forty-fifth birthday.

Although she often paints outside, Jennifer also has the luxury of this large studio. Having multiple tables is especially handy because you can allow fabrics to dry on one table while you start creating another project on the next table.

TIP
Collect general supplies and have them handy so you don't have to hunt for them when you're in a creative mood.

Your Workspace

Your mood can affect the outcome of your work, so why not crank up your favorite music, turn up the lights, and open a window for fresh air? Wear old, comfortable clothing, and don't forget to put on old shoes. And, while you're at it, why not decorate your studio/workspace so it's an area in which you enjoy spending time?

To protect your workspace, we recommend you cover the tables and floor with plastic or vinyl. You can buy drop cloths at a hardware store or inexpensive vinyl by the yard in some fabric stores.

Clean Up

Store all of your paint and dye supplies in closed containers in a cool, dry place. They will remain usable for several years. Once mixed with water, dyes and paints should be used within a few days. It is safe to pour small amounts of leftover paint or dye down the drain. Thoroughly wash your containers and tools with warm, soapy water right after use and let them air dry.

WORKSPACE TIPS

- If you are working on a dark table, such as dark wood, cover it with white plastic (versus clear), so the true color of the dye or paint can be seen. You can also slip a piece of white fabric under a clear piece of plastic.
- If using a "good" table as the work surface, secure plastic by taping it to the underside of the table. Then tape the fabric on top of the plastic.
- If you are using an "old" surface that will not be used for anything other than fabric painting, secure plastic by stapling it to the underside of the table. Then secure the fabric on top of the plastic with tacks.
- Wipe the plastic surface with a damp sponge between projects.
- If your table is especially rough or uneven, first cover it with plywood or stiff cardboard cut to fit, and then plastic as indicated above.

Jennifer's mother, Jane Varcoe, paints 80 percent of her fabric outdoors on huge tables set in her beautiful yard and garden. Weather permitting, you can duplicate Jane's ideal setting by making an outdoor table with two sawhorses and a large piece of plywood. Photograph by Mark Horton.

Safety

If used properly, the dyes, paints, and auxiliary products most commonly used in the fiber art industry generally are safe and non-toxic. There is no need to be afraid of working with any of the products mentioned in this book; however, we recommend you follow these tips:

- Always read and make sure you understand the manufacturers' instructions that come with a product. If not, contact the manufacturer.

- Always avoid breathing powdered dyes or auxiliary powders by wearing a dust mask or respirator. Once a chemical or dye is in a solution, you can remove the mask.

- If you are pregnant, do not handle dye powders or any chemicals. Have someone else mix the dye and soda ash into a solution for you.

- Wear gloves to protect your hands from constant exposure to chemicals.

- If you use kitchen utensils or containers, donate them to your workroom; do not return them to the kitchen.

- Do not eat or smoke in your work area or areas where the products are stored.

- Protect your work area with plastic or vinyl, and if there is a spill, wipe it up immediately.

- Keep all chemicals clearly labeled and out of the reach of children. Store them in a cool, dry location.

SECTION 2
Dyes

Black Tulips, 25" x 29", 1997, by Anne Anderson. The foundation for this impressive piece of fiber art is cotton, while the rest of the fabric is silk that Anne painted with Procion H reactive dyes. It is created with the Snippet technique and is featured in More Snippet Sensations. More of Anne's extraordinary work can be viewed at her website, www.Anneanderson.com.

Different types of dyes.

Types of Dyes

There are many different types of dye categories, or classes. The two most common dye classes used today by textile artists are acid (wool and silk) and reactive dyes (cotton and silk). When properly fixed, both produce vibrant, brilliant colors and are light fast and washable. Most of the projects in this book use a reactive dye.

Polyester uses its own unique type of dye known as disperse dye. Even though disperse dye will dye cotton, it isn't recommended for the fiber artist because it doesn't produce brilliant colors and isn't as colorfast as reactive dyes.

It is important also to mention natural dyes. They are once again becoming popular after taking a back seat to synthetic dyes, which were discovered in the mid-nineteenth century.

Because dyeing textiles is an ancient art with endless techniques—including tub immersion, gradation, direct, batik, tie-dye, and Shibori—many simple and complicated recipes have been developed over the past 2,000 years. Along with these techniques, many different auxiliary products have also been developed, such as fixing agents, color removers, dye thickeners, and surface modifiers. This book simplifies the process of dyeing for you by introducing a few basic techniques that you can do at home.

Please remember that all dyes need fixing, either by a dye-activating chemical such as soda ash (also referred to as Dye-activator™, potash, and washing soda) or by the heat and moisture of steam. Carefully read the package instructions included with the brand of dye you purchase.

The next few pages will give you a little more information about reactive, acid, and natural dyes.

My Three Amigos, 51" x 46", 2001, by Melody Johnson. Melody dyed cottons and silk charmeuse with Procion MX dyes, using the direct dyeing method. To view more of her remarkable quilts visit her website at www.artfabrik.com.

Reactive Dyes

These dyes are of great value to fiber artists because they do not require the use of complicated fixing agents to color a large range of natural fibers, such as cotton, linen, hemp, flax, paper, and reeds. Reactive dyes are synthetic and are so named because they react chemically at a molecular level, forming a dye-fiber bond. They require an alkaline for fixing, such as soda ash. The activator is either dissolved in warm water before being added to the dye bath or, in the direct dye technique, the fabric is first soaked in the dissolved activa-

tor and then dyed. A small percentage of fiber artists prefers a hot-water H reactive dye. The most-used dye by fiber artists is a cold-water MX Reactive dye. The most common brand name for H and MX Reactive dyes is Procion™ (manufactured by DyStar). The dye gives you brilliant colors, is easy to use, and is the dye we use most often throughout this book.

Different brands of dyes require varied application methods, temperature of the dye bath, and curing methods or time. Carefully follow package instructions.

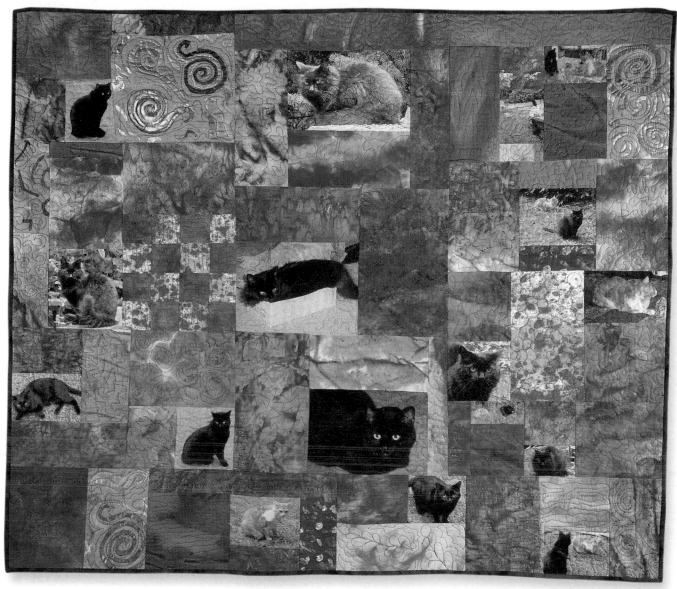

Kitties for Theresa, 51" x 51", 2001, by Cindy Walter. Cindy made this quilt as a Christmas present for her "cat crazy" daughter-in-law, Theresa. She simply photographed the family cats with a digital camera and then printed them on her inkjet printer using Print on Cotton paper, made by Jacquard (inkjet printers use acid dyes). She painted the fabric between the cat photos with Dye-Na-Flow paint.

Acid Dyes

This is a large category of industrial dyes, which gets its name because it needs acidic conditions, such as a vinegar bath, to fix the dye to the fiber. Acid dyes are used for animal fibers, including fur, feathers, wool, and silk, as well as nylon, even though it isn't a natural fiber. Acid dyes are extremely predictable and are available in a wide range of colors. They are most important to the fiber artist to dye wool.

All dyes used in inkjet desktop printers are acid dyes. They work beautifully on silk if you follow the steam fix instruction (see page 21). We suggest buying pre-packaged silks or cottons that are mounted on release paper to feed it through your printer. The cotton is treated with a mordant, which enables the acid dye to adhere to its fibers.

This beautiful rug was dyed with Pre-Reduced Natural Indigo Dye from Jacquard. Photo courtesy of Rupert, Gibbon & Spider, Inc.

Natural Dyes

Many people love natural dyes because of their earthy subtleties and ecological attraction. Although natural dyes have unique purposes, for the most part they are not as brilliant or wash-fast as synthetic dyes. Most natural dyes are known as "adjective" dyes, meaning they require a strong mordant, such as alum, to fix them to the fibers. Many different types of mordant are used to set natural dyes, each producing different results. The use of a mordant adds complicated steps to the natural dyeing process, and many mordants are made from heavy metals and can be toxic.

One natural dye worth exploring is indigo blue. This dye has played an important role in several cultures throughout history (for example, the famous Blue Men of Morocco are a North African tribe who dress from head to toe in indigo-dyed fabric), and a vast number of books are devoted to it. It produces the familiar blue of blue jean pants. We found indigo dyes to be expensive and very time-consuming to prepare. The dye is not water-soluble, so it needs to be reduced chemically in sodium hydrosulfate and lye. Fortunately, we discovered a wonderful new product called Pre-Reduced Natural Indigo Dye, made by Jacquard, which is easy to use and provides the same unique results as regular indigo ink. You only need to add Sodium Hydrosulfite and soda ash, and it takes about 10 minutes to prepare the dye bath.

As you can see, the types of dyes available, and techniques used, are nearly endless. In the following sections we provide a few simple dyeing projects to get you started. Because we are dyeing silk and cotton in our projects, we are using reactive dyes. If you plan to dye wool you should use an acid dye. When you are ready to learn more about dyes, please refer to the books in the Recommended Reading section (page 94). We hope we have sparked a desire in you to explore the wonderful world of dyes!

Indigo dye plant. This plant produces a highly sought-after rich blue dye. Photo courtesy of Rupert, Gibbon & Spider, Inc.

Tranquility, 24" x 24", 1999, by Veronica "Ronnie" Martin. The painting "July Sunlight," by Douglas Grey, inspired Ronnie to create this project in a Snippet class taught by Cindy Walter in New Zealand. A talented fiber artist, Ronnie enjoys hand-dyeing her own fabric with Procion MX for most of her projects. This quilt was shown in Cindy's book, More Snippet Sensations. Photograph by Jeff Mein Smith, New Zealand.

Methods of Dyeing

TIP

If you are mixing colors, be sure to mix enough to complete your project, because it is difficult to re-create exact shades, or measure the dye and keep notes as you go so you can re-create the recipe. Jennifer keeps a Rolodex in her work area to write down her recipe concoctions.

When using reactive dyes there are two basic methods of applying it to fabric: immersion bath and direct application. In either method, there are endless techniques—and many more yet to be discovered. The immersion dyeing method produces fabric that is more solid in color, such as background dyeing or gradation dyeing, by submerging the fabric in a dye bath. The direct dyeing method produces an array of patterned or multi-colored fabrics by adding the dye directly on top of the fabric.

A popular dyeing technique is called "resist," which simply means anything that prevents the dye from penetrating the fabric. You can create a resist pattern by tightly tying, pleating, overstitching, or twisting the fabric, such as in Shibori or tie-dye. To prevent the dye from blending (bleeding) together or penetrating certain areas of the fabric, you could also apply a resist substance to the fabric, like wax or gutta.

On the following pages we show you how to use the immersion and direct methods of dyeing with a variety of techniques.

Fixing Dyes

All dyes need to be fixed by either adding dye-activating chemicals to the dye bath or by the heat of steaming once dyed. The most commonly used dye-activator is soda ash; however, similar products, such as potash, washing soda, and Dye-activator™, are also used. A few newer manufacturer-premixed types of dyes, like Silk Colors Green Label liquid dye, only require a rinse in Permanent Dyeset Concentrate at the end of the process. Before you begin using a new dye, carefully read the package instructions.

Chemical Fixing

To chemically fix the dye follow one of these simple directions:

Immersion dyeing: Dissolve ¼ cup of soda ash in 1 quart of hot tap water. Then, add the dissolved soda ash to the finished dye bath in intervals while stirring. Do not pour directly onto the fabric in the dye bath because it can cause blotches.

Direct dyeing method: Dissolve ¼ cup of soda ash in 1 quart of hot tap water. Prepare enough of this liquid so the fabric can be completely immersed. Soak the fabric in the soda ash water for 10 minutes. Remove the fabric and wring out excess liquid. The fabric is now ready for dye painting.

Direct dyeing method with Permanent Dyeset Concentrate and Jacquard Silk Colors Green Label dyes: Put the dyed piece of fabric into a Dyeset solution of 1 ounce Dyeset per quart of water and agitate vigorously for 30 seconds. Continue stirring for 4 to 5 minutes. Do not let the fabric sit in the Dyeset concentrate. Remove the fabric from the Dyeset and rinse again with mild soap and water until the water runs clear.

Steaming

If you can steam vegetables, you can steam fabric! Smaller pieces of fabric can be steamed at home using a "homemade" steamer, as described here. If you are working with large pieces of fabric, you can purchase a large commercial steamer or a smaller stovetop variety; although costly, they are very efficient.

1 Roll the fabric in white newsprint or kraft paper. Make sure there is a layer

Steaming Pot

Foil Dome

Fabric Bundle

Rack

Water

Heat Source

of paper between each layer of fabric so that one layer of fabric does not touch another layer and there are no wrinkles. It is important to take the time to do this properly.

2 When all of the fabric has been rolled, wrap additional paper around the outside of the bundle. Tape the bundle securely. Gently coil the bundle like a donut to make it small enough to fit in the pot without touching the sides.

3 Pour water into the pot so the rack sits well above the water line and the rack remains dry. Place the rack into the pot. Place the bundle of fabric on the rack.

4 Shape a piece of aluminum foil into a dome and place it over the bundle to protect the fabric from condensation (you want the condensation from the lid to drip on the aluminum foil and not onto the bundle of fabric). Again, make sure the bundle and the foil do not touch the sides of the pot.

5 Cover the pot with the lid and bring the water to a boil. Reduce heat and steam for 1 hour. Make sure the pot does not boil dry. If you need to add water, use something with a long spout like a watering can so you do not get water on the fabric. Allow the bundle to cool. Unwrap. Rinse in cool water until the water is clear of excess dye.

Fixing a Combination of Dye and Paint

It is possible to mix dyes and paints on the same piece of cloth. To fix the combined colorants, first iron the fabric to set the paint, then steam according to the above directions to set the dye.

These are the general supplies you need for immersion dyeing.

Dyeing Techniques

Immersion Dyeing

Use the immersion dyeing method when you want to dye a piece of fabric all one color. The depth of color is achieved by how much dye powered is used (a pinch to several tablespoons), the amount of water, and the length of time in the dye bath. These instructions are a guideline because they vary between types of dyes and by their manufacturers. Read and follow the package instructions for the type of dye you purchase. (**Note:** In immersion dyeing, fabric is dampened before it is added to the dye bath to ensure even coloring of the fabric, but it must not be soaking wet, because excess water can dilute the dye bath.)

1 Machine-wash the fabric on the hot cycle with 1 tablespoon Synthrapol. Keep the fabric damp, or re-dampen before using. If you are using PFD fabric, it is not necessary to pre-wash the fabric; simply dampen. Be sure to wring out all of the excess water because soaking wet fabric can dilute the dye solution.

2 Mix dye solutions: Put on rubber gloves and the dust mask. In the 2-cup measuring container, dissolve the MX Reactive dye powder in ¼ cup of warm water. See ratios for different colors on the following page. Stir until the dye powder is completely dissolved, creating a paste, and then add more water to make 1 cup of dye, or dye solution.

Hibiscus, 20" x 18", 1996, by Diana Morrison. Diana used hand-dyed fabrics from Shades Textiles to create this remarkable piece of fabric art. The beautiful fabrics dyed with Procion MX reactive dyes and the immersion technique provide shadowing and create an effect of sunlight playing on the petals. This piece is featured in Cindy's book, Snippet Sensations.

3 Mix 3 gallons of warm tap water (105 degrees) and the 1 cup of dissolved dye solution in the 5-gallon bucket. **Note:** If desired, add ½ cup of salt per gallon of water at this stage to help set the dye.

4 Immerse the damp fabric into the dye bath.

5 Stir the dye bath for 5 minutes to ensure the dye solution reaches all surfaces of the fabric and the fabric is fully immersed in the dye. This is very important for even color; the fabric must stay immersed the entire time. Then stir every few minutes for the next 20 minutes.

6 Dissolve ¼ cup of soda ash in a quart of hot tap water.

7 Slowly, in intervals while stirring, add the dissolved soda ash (the dye-activator) to the dye bath. Do not pour it directly on the fabric. Continue to stir for 1 minute every 10 minutes, for 1 hour.

8 To achieve maximum color absorption, keep the fabric immersed in the dye bath for 1 hour after the activator is added,

Dye Powder Needed to Make 3 Gallons of Dye Bath to Dye 3 Yards of Fabric

These calculations are to create a medium shade of the indicated color. You can create a lighter or darker shade by adjusting the amount of dye powder by just a few pinches.

Color	# of Tablespoons
Lights: yellow, orange, pink	1
Mediums: blue, green, red	2
Darks: black, navy	3

½ hour for pastels. Stir frequently to ensure the fabric is evenly colored. **Note:** Even though this is the amount of time recommended by manufacturers, Jennifer feels she achieves more brilliant colors by leaving the fabric in the dye bath up to 4 hours.

9 Remove the fabric from the dye bath. Rinse in cool water until there is no dye color left in the water. Finally, wash in warm water with Synthrapol to remove any unfixed dye molecules.

10 Machine-dry on a normal setting.

TIP
You can create a variety of patterned fabrics (that are not solid in color) by adding the dissolved soda ash solution later or directly on top of the fabric, scrunching the fabric up in the dye bath, or by not stirring.

TIP
If the fabric is too light, a second cup of dye solution can be added at any time during the procedure.

A Touch of Van Gogh, 35" x 28", 1997, by Cindy Water. Cindy wanted to create a rendition of Van Gogh's "Starry Night" painting. To capture the essence of his painting, the first thing was to select the correct fabric colors. She chose a variety of gradation-dyed fabrics from Alaska Dyeworks and used a commercially printed batik for the border. This project appears in Cindy's book, More Snippet Sensations.

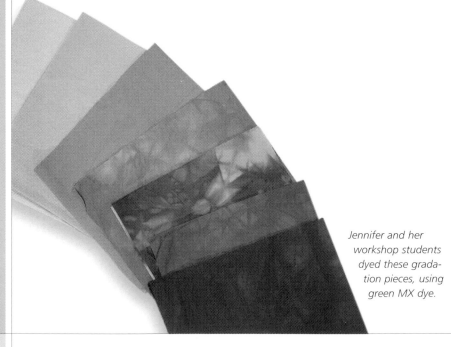

Jennifer and her workshop students dyed these gradation pieces, using green MX dye.

Victoria Barnett, owner of Alaska Dyeworks, shares these tips:

- Take procedure notes whenever you dye fabric and save a swatch of the fabric with the notes.
- Follow good safety procedures.
- Clean up right away.
- Use the best grade cotton you can afford.
- Test a new dye before using.
- Don't be afraid to try odd color combinations.

Gradation Project

Gradation dyeing has always been a popular form of immersion dyeing for quilters. The following instructions are for eight gradations of one color using ½-yard lengths of fabric and MX Reactive dye. Each value level is dyed in its own dye bucket. This is the method of gradation dyeing taught by Joyce Mori and Jan Myers-Newbury in their book, *Dye It! Paint It! Quilt It!*.

1 Machine-wash the fabric on the hot cycle with 1 tablespoon Synthrapol. Keep the fabric damp, or re-dampen before using. If you are using PFD fabric, it is not necessary to pre-wash the fabric; simply dampen. Be sure to wring out all of the excess water because soaking wet fabric can dilute the dye solution.

2 Put on rubber gloves and the dust mask. In the 2-cup measuring container, dissolve the dye powder in ¼ cup warm water. The amount of dye powder varies depending on the color of dye (see the measurements above). Stir until the powder is completely dissolved, forming a dye paste. Then add enough water to this dye paste to make 2 cups of dye solution.

3 In an 8-ounce container, thoroughly dissolve 2 tablespoons of soda ash in 1 cup of hot water. Prepare eight of these cups. Set a cup of the dissolved soda ash solution next to each of the eight large dye buckets. You may now remove your dust mask.

4 Pour 1 gallon of warm water into each dye bucket. All buckets should contain water that is approximately the same temperature to ensure smooth, even gradations.

5 Add ½ cup of salt to each dye bucket and stir until dissolved.

6 Have a gallon container of room-temperature water available. You are starting with 2 cups of dye solution. Measure out 1 cup of the dye solution and pour it into the first bucket. This is your darkest value. You now have 1 cup of dye solution left in the 2-cup measuring container. Add 1 cup of room-temperature water to this remaining dye solution to once again create

2 cups of dye solution (half as strong as the dye solution that went into the first bucket). Stir the dye solution and then put 1 cup of this new solution into the second bucket. Now add 1 cup of room-temperature water to the remaining dye solution to once again create 2 cups of slightly diluted dye solution. Continue this process, putting 1 cup of dye solution into the bucket and then replacing it with water, until you have added dye to all eight buckets. You will be left with one cup of very light dye solution, which may be discarded. Stir each bucket.

7 Add a ½-yard piece of dampened fabric to the first dye bucket. Stir for 5 minutes with your gloved hands and push out any air bubbles. Keep the fabric submerged. Add fabric to the second dye bucket and repeat the stirring process. When all of the fabric has been added to its respective bucket and stirred, set the timer for 10 minutes. Thoroughly stir each dye bucket for about 1 minute every 10 minutes, for the next 30 minutes (for a total of three stirrings).

8 Add the dissolved soda ash solution (from Step 3) to each bucket. Do not pour the solution directly on the fabric. Stir each bucket for 1 minute. Set the timer for 10 minutes. Thoroughly stir each dye bucket every 10 minutes for the next 60 minutes (for a total of six stirrings).

9 Remove the fabric from the dye buckets at the end of the process. Thoroughly rinse the fabric in cool water to remove the excess dye solution.

10 Machine-wash the fabrics in hot water and 2 tablespoons of Synthrapol. Machine-dry on normal setting.

Dye Powder Needed to Make Dye Bath for 8-Step Gradation Dyeing	
These calculations are to create a medium shade of the indicated color.	
Color	**# of Tablespoons**
Lights: yellow, orange, pink	2
Mediums: blue, green, red	4
Darks: black, navy	6

- 4 yards 100-percent natural cotton, cut into ½-yard lengths
- MX Reactive dye, any color
- Synthrapol
- Soda ash
- Eight 2- to 5-gallon plastic buckets
- 2-cup gradated measuring cup with pouring spout
- 1-gallon measuring container (such as a milk jug)
- Plastic measuring tablespoon
- Plastic spoons for mixing
- Eight 8-ounce plastic containers (such as yogurt or deli containers)
- Timer
- Rubber gloves
- Dust mask
- Paper towels
- 4 cups of salt

Alaska Dyeworks is a dyeing company known for producing beautifully gradated and tie-dyed fabrics with MX dyes.

Direct dyeing is very easy. It is similar to watercolor painting, where the colors flow together, producing beautiful blended results. Play for a while, remembering there is no such thing as an ugly piece of fabric.

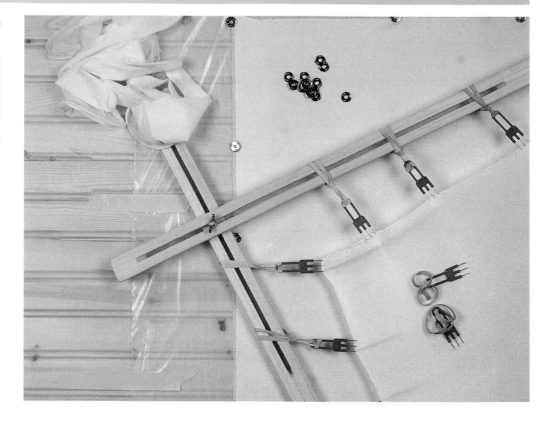

If you do not want the dye colors to bleed together, you must use lines of wax or "gutta resist" between the colors and stretch the fabric on a wooden frame so it is suspended above the table with tacks or hooks.

Deborah Padrich created this summer top using resist between the colors of dye. Photo courtesy of Rupert, Gibbon & Spider, Inc.

Direct Dyeing

There are endless ways you can apply dye directly to fabric. The direct application of dye onto prepared fabric is a simple and easy way to dye your own fabric. A random application of dye produces a spectacular kaleidoscope of color. In this method, dye is rolled, brushed, poured, spattered, or sponged onto the fabric. The techniques mentioned in the painting section of this book can also be used with dyes, but just be sure to follow the dye fixing procedure.

You can also produce a more specific motif with crisp lines by painting with a brush after you have applied a product called "resist" to the fabric to prevent the dyes from running together.

You might like the results of painting with a dye that is thicker in consistency. To achieve this you will have to add a thickener to the dye. Thickeners are made from such things as seaweed, starch, and gum

tannins, and are produced under the commercial names of Sodium Alginate, No Flow, and Superclear.

The method of application you choose dictates the supplies you need. You can either work on a flat surface, or stretch the fabric on a frame. If you want to produce random patterns, a color-wash effect, or tied Shibori, then you only need a covered flat surface to lay the fabric on. If you are painting a motif and want clean lines, then a stretcher frame (and gutta resist) must be used to prevent the dyes from spreading and blending into each other. The list on the opposite page is a general list for all direct dyeing techniques; adapt it to your specific project.

The following sections teach you how to direct dye with powdered and liquid dyes, as well as how to use resists.

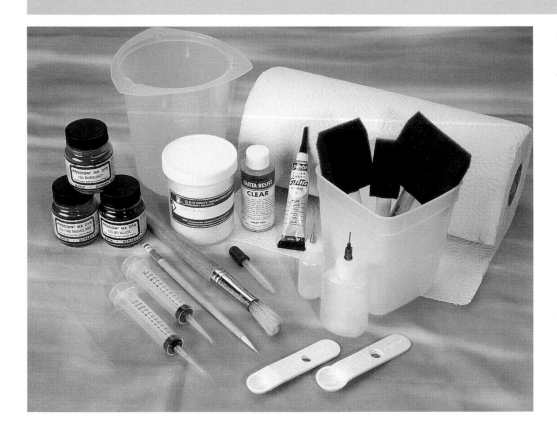

These are the general supplies you need for direct dyeing.

To Use MX Reactive Dyes in the Direct Dyeing Method

1 Use PFD fabric or machine-wash the fabric on the hot cycle with 1 tablespoon Synthrapol. Allow the fabric to dry.

2 Mix dye solutions: Put on rubber gloves and the dust mask. In a 1-cup measuring container, dissolve the dye powder in ⅛ cup of warm water; this is the dye paste. Stir and then add more water to make ⅓ cup of dye. The amount of dye powder varies depending on the color of dye and intensity of the result you are trying to achieve. See the box at right for approximately how much dye powder you will need to make ⅓ cup of a medium-strength dye solution.

3 Dissolve the soda ash according to the package instructions. Presoak the fabric in the solution for 10 minutes.

4 Apply the dye by either painting with a brush or sponge or spraying it from a bottle.*

Dye Powder Needed to Make ⅓ Cup of Dye Solution

These calculations are to create a medium shade of the indicated color.

Color	# of Teaspoons
Lights: yellow, orange, pink	1
Mediums: blue, green, red	2
Darks: black, navy	3

5 Let fabric cure overnight. Then thoroughly rinse the fabric in warm water to remove the excess dye solution until the water runs clear. Machine-wash in hot water and 1 tablespoon of Synthrapol.

6 Machine-dry on normal setting or air dry.

*Numerous application methods are presented throughout the rest of this section. All of them are fun; try several on the same piece of fabric!

YOU WILL NEED

- Cotton or silk fabric
- Synthrapol
- MX Reactive dyes or liquid dye such as Jacquard Silk Colors**, any colors
- Soda ash (for use with MX Reactive dyes)
- Steaming equipment or Permanent Dyeset Concentrate (for use with Silk Colors)
- Several containers of water to dilute dyes and to rinse brushes
- 1-cup measuring container
- Assortment of plastic mixing containers (such as yogurt or deli containers)
- Bucket
- Plastic spoons for measuring and mixing (teaspoon)
- Optional: frame and tacks
- Assortment of brushes (foam, bamboo, natural, and synthetic bristles)
- Additional applicators (sponges, syringes, eyedroppers, spray bottle, stamps, etc.)
- Optional: gutta resist, sea salt
- Rubber gloves
- Dust mask
- Paper towels

** MX Reactive dyes and Silk Colors are used differently, but either can be used for direct dyeing techniques.

Life's a Bowl of Fruit, 2000, 35" x 35", by Celia Buchanan. With a Masters of Art degree from the City University of London, this talented Scotland-born fiber artist used Jacquard Silk Colors to create this brilliant scarf. She says, "I like Jacquard Silk Colors because it is an intense, rich, and truly transparent color that flows freely on the silk. I have a degree of flexibility with the intensity of the shade as it can be used either full strength or diluted with water. It is the perfect partner for silk." She used black gutta resist to define the lines of the motif on silk crepe de chine. Celia's work has been published in several books and articles. She teaches seminars on silk painting and fiber arts; for more information visit her website at www.celiabuchanan.com. Photo courtesy of Rupert, Gibbon & Spider, Inc.

TIP

Silk Colors Green Label has taken dyeing fabric to a new level for the fiber artist of the twenty-first century. Simply apply this dye to PFD fabric, then rinse in Permanent Dyeset Concentrate. What could be easier? Look at the scarf on page 28; you can achieve these intense, beautiful colors.

We created this handsome tie and scarf using Silk Colors and a kit by Jacquard. We simply painted the dye on the fabric and allowed the colors to bleed together.

To Use Jacquard Silk Colors in the Direct Dyeing Method

We love using a pre-mixed liquid dye called Silk Colors™ by Jacquard. It already contains the fixtant, and the fabric does not need to be presoaked in soda ash. The Silk Colors Red Label only has to be steamed for 30 to 40 minutes once finished to set the dye. The Silk Colors also has a Green Label that doesn't have to be steamed; it can be set by using Permanent Dyeset Concentrate. In this instance, once the project is finished, soak it for 5 minutes in a solution of Permanent Dyeset Concentrate and water (be sure to follow the manufacturer's instructions).

1 Use PFD fabric or machine-wash the fabric on the hot cycle with 1 tablespoon Synthrapol. Allow the fabric to air dry. You do not need to pre-treat the fabric with salt, dye activator, or soda ash.

2 Apply dye in any manner desired. (See the following pages for inspiration.)

3 If using Silk Colors Red Label, steam to permanently set the dye. If using Silk Colors Green Label, steam or rinse afterwards in Permanent Dyeset Concentrate. See setting instructions on page 21.

Brushes are important and need care! Wash them thoroughly after each use. Occasionally, a small amount of paint or dye can hide up in the bristles. Be very careful about this because a spot of the wrong color might ruin your project. Fiber artist Kim Meyer says, "I keep my brushes separated for use with different mediums and by color family in each medium."

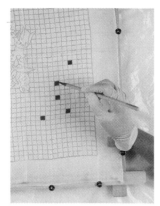

This scarf comes pre-stamped with gutta resist by the manufacturer; all you have to do is paint in the colors with dye.

This scarf was pre-stamped with gutta resist by the manufacturer, Jacquard. There are many pre-stamped designs available. Diana Thorp beautifully painted each section with dye.

YOU WILL NEED

- Silk scarf
- Synthrapol
- Design idea or large picture to trace
- Jacquard Silk Colors Green Label, any colors
- Gutta resist
- Small bottle with medium tip
- Assortment of plastic mixing containers (such as yogurt containers)
- Eyedropper
- Small tipped brushes
- Stretcher frame or embroidery hoop
- Silk tacks or claws
- Container of water to dilute dyes and to rinse brushes
- Rubber gloves
- Paper towels

Direct Dye Painting Using Gutta Resist

If you were to paint on silk or cotton with dyes, the colors would bleed together, creating a beautifully blended, or watercolor, effect. If you want to paint a specific image, or keep crisp lines between the colors, you must use a line of resist between the colors to prevent them from touching one another. Several products are used as a resist, including wax and gutta. While wax is commonly used and is widely available, we love to use "gutta" resist, which comes in clear, gold, and black, because it is easy to apply. The gold or black color of the gutta remains on the silk once finished, resembling stained glass.

1 Use PFD fabric or machine-wash the silk on the warm cycle with 1 tablespoon of Synthrapol. Allow to air dry.

2 Place the silk on the frame by stretching it tightly on the stretcher bars and securing it with silk tacks about every 2 inches. Begin pinning on one side and work your way around the frame. Put the tacks in the very edge of the fabric so the tack marks will not leave a hole. The fabric must be taut and be suspended above the work surface.

3 Pour a small amount of gutta resist into the dispenser bottle with a medium-sized tip. (**Note:** Some brands of gutta come in a tube with a built-in dispenser tip.) If you are using a pattern as a guideline for your motif, center it under the stretched fabric. Trace the pattern with the gutta, or trace with a pencil and then go over the pencil lines with gutta. Draw on your design with thin lines of gutta resist, to separate each area of color. When you paint your dye in each area, it will spread on the silk until it reaches the resist line.

4 After you have applied the gutta, hold the silk up to the light and look from the back to make sure the gutta has penetrated all of the way through and that there aren't any breaks in the lines. If there are breaks or the gutta has not fully penetrated the silk, carefully apply more gutta.

5 Allow the gutta to thoroughly dry, approximately 30 minutes. The thicker the gutta, the longer the drying time needed.

6 Mix the dye to achieve desired colors. Use an eyedropper and place a small amount of each color into the plastic containers. Be careful not to splash the dye.

7 Apply dye to the appropriate areas with a small brush. Dip your brush gently into a color. Paint all areas by touching the brush to the fabric about ½ inch from the gutta line. It will migrate the rest of the way. For large areas, work quickly, painting the color from corner to corner. For consistency, always paint the entire section; adding dye to an area that has already dried will produce different results.

8 Let dry 24 hours. Set the dye by following the steaming technique or rinsing in Permanent Dyeset Concentrate. See setting instructions on page 21.

Clear gutta resist leaves white lines (or clear spaces) between the color. You can add dye to clear gutta to create a colored gutta of your choice. This scarf was created using Silk Colors Green Label and clear gutta resist. Photo courtesy of Rupert, Gibbon & Spider, Inc.

Wax is most commonly used in the batiking technique. The dye cannot penetrate the area where it was applied; when wax washes away, white lines are left between the colors. This shirt was created using wax and Jacquard MX Dye. Photo courtesy of Rupert, Gibbon & Spider, Inc.

Black gutta resist outlines the colors with a stained glass effect. This shirt was created using Silk Colors Green Label. Photo courtesy of Rupert, Gibbon & Spider, Inc.

TIP

Hold the gutta bottle like a pencil. Gently squeeze the bottle on a paper towel to remove bubbles until the resist begins to flow smoothly, creating continuous lines. The lines must connect or the dye will bleed though the gaps in the gutta. We suggest you work with a medium tip for your first projects; however, using small, medium, or large tips in the dispenser bottle to apply the gutta will produce different thicknesses of lines.

Elle Markusen created this stunning Arashi Shibori silk sculpture by wrapping the silk around a pole before dyeing. In the past 80 years she has experimented with all types of fiber art, but she especially enjoys painting dye on 100-percent silk. She used Sennelier Tinfix dye from France for the projects on this page. In the private collection of Tom and Mary Markusen.

FROM JENNIFER

I was first introduced to the world of fabric painting—when I was just 7 years old—by my Uncle Tom. His mother, Elle Markusen, is a fiber artist who created the pieces on this page. One summer, Elle, Uncle Tom, and my Aunt Mary set up a painting studio for my three cousins and me. I still vividly picture their front yard strewn with fabric, an electric frying pan (for hot wax), and a variety of brushes and homemade stamps. I'll never forget the absolute joy of freely painting for hours with the warm sun on our backs and the birds chirping in the trees. All of us kids felt the excitement of achievement; we had suddenly become artists! I will always be thankful to my uncle and aunt for inspiring in me a desire to explore the world of fiber arts.

Shibori and Tie-dyeing

Shibori is an ancient Japanese art form. You can create an endless variety of patterns on fabric using different methods of folding, sewing seams, and even wrapping the fabric around different objects. Shibori and tie-dyeing are similar and both are forms of the dye-resist process that prevents the dye from reaching the entire surface of the fabric.

Use only two or three colors of dye on your first Shibori project; we used yellow and red in the example on the following page. When you are ready to experiment, work with a multitude of colors. Remember that the dyes will bleed together, so you may end up with "muddy" colors.

Rising Sun, 1992, 18" x 22", by Elle Markusen.

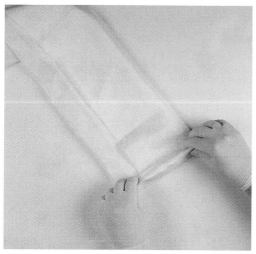
Step 2

Step 3

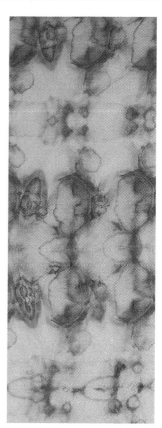

This striking scarf was created using only two colors of dye and a common method of Shibori.

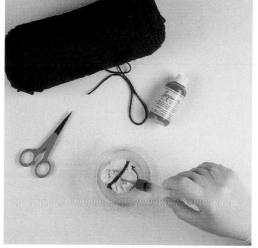
Step 5

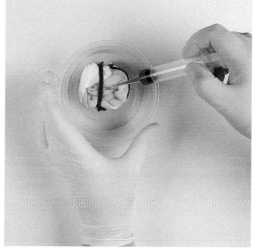
Step 6

Shibori Scarf

1 Use PFD silk, or machine-wash the silk on the hot cycle with 1 tablespoon Synthrapol. Allow to air dry. **Note:** Silk works best for this Shibori method.

2 Roll-hem the scarf on all four sides. Fold the fabric so it is very long but only about 6 inches wide.

3 Starting at one end, roll the fabric to create a tight tube. Now roll the tight tube into a ball.

4 Wrap the ball tightly with yarn or string; tie. Place the ball in the plastic container.

5 Fill a syringe full of the lightest color of dye. Disperse the color around the ball.

6 Rinse the syringe with water then fill it with the second color of dye. Aiming for the white areas, disperse the second color throughout the ball.

7 Allow the ball to dry overnight.

8 Rinse in Permanent Dyeset Concentrate, according to the setting instructions on page 21.

9 Dry in any manner.

YOU WILL NEED
- 12- x 44-inch piece of silk
- Synthrapol
- Jacquard Silk Colors Green Label, any colors
- Syringe or eyedropper
- String and scissors
- Small plastic container to hold ball of fabric
- Assortment of small plastic mixing containers (such as yogurt containers)
- Cup of water to rinse syringe or eyedropper
- Gloves
- Paper towels
- Permanent Dyeset Concentrate or steaming equipment
- Needle and thread

Discharge Methods and Variations on Techniques

As was stated earlier, there is an endless number of techniques to apply dyes and many variations in each technique. Some of our favorite variations include salting, discharge, potato dextrin resist, and even using ink as a dye. Remember to experiment!

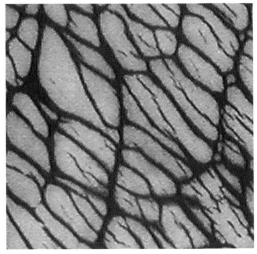

Procion MX dye and potato dextrin. Photo courtesy of Rupert, Gibbon & Spider, Inc.

Potato Dextrin Resist

Potato and corn dextrin have become popular with textile designers because they enable the artist to temporarily modify the surface of the fabric prior to the application of the dye. Both products shrink and crack on the fabric, creating an unusual veined pattern when the dye is applied. First soak the fabric in the dextrin, allow it to completely dry, and then apply the dye.

Kim Meyer created this attractive velvet discharge scarf using the kit shown below by Jacquard. Photo courtesy of Rupert, Gibbon & Spider, Inc.

Velvet Discharge

Once velvet is dyed, the dye can be removed in patterns using discharge paste from Jacquard or PROChem. Using the immersion technique, dye the velvet black or other color of choice. Let the fabric completely dry. Paint the desired pattern on the velvet with the discharge paste. Let the paste completely dry. Going outdoors where there is fresh air, steam iron the backside of the scarf for several seconds in each area. Do not breath the discharge fumes. The Jacquard kit pictured at left includes everything you need—even the scarf!

Placing Salt on Wet Dye

Look at the beautiful affect salt can have on dyed silk (above). Simply sprinkle rock salt on top of the cotton or silk before the dye has dried. As the fabric dries, the salt will cause a rippling effect. Small sea salt and large rock salt will create different results.

Direct Scrunch Dyeing

The scrunch dyeing technique is one of the fastest methods to creatively use dye. Jennifer created silk for the cover-up at left by applying dye to the silk while it was scrunched in a pile. Leave it scrunched until the silk is dry. For directions on making this cover-up, see page 93. Also refer to Scrunch Painting, page 46.

Emerald Reflection, 2001, 86" x 86", by Sharon Schamber. Sharon used All-purpose Ink and Fantastix, both from Tsukineko (see below), to paint this stunning quilt, which has been shown in Quilter Newsletter *and* Quiltmaker *magazines. Prior to designing quilts, Sharon was the head designer and owner of a business that created upscale wedding and pageant gowns. This background gave her the skills for fine hand, machine, and bead work. In her first competition attempt in 1999, she won the Jinny Beyer Borders on Brilliance contest at the Houston International Quilt Show. Sharon is a skilled teacher and designer; she can be reached at schamber@easilink.com.*

One final important type of dye we should mention is all-purpose ink. These inks work similar to dyes except that you simply set them with the heat of an iron to fix the ink when you are finished. To use the ink, dip a Fantastix stick lightly into the ink and brush the ink onto the fabric. Heat set with the iron. Set the project between colors if you do not want them to blend. Photo courtesy Tsukineko.

1930 Tulip Bouquet, 40" x 40", 2001, by Cindy Walter and Gail Baker Rowe. Cindy and Gail recreated this 1930 appliqué pattern with Fabrics To Dye For fabrics for their new book, Basic Appliqué, 1930s Patterns Created With Traditional and Contemporary Techniques *(2002, Krause Publications). Hand-dyed or -painted fabrics are a perfect complement for traditional patterns.*

SECTION 3
Paints

Painting is one of the easiest methods by which a fiber artist can color fabrics. The first thing you must realize is even though the process of applying paint to fabric is easy and enjoyable, the final outcome is not always what you might have expected when you started out because of weather conditions, the paint to water ratio, and the type of fabric used will vary the results. We suggest you approach fabric painting as an adventure and be prepared to enjoy the results, even when they do not turn out as expected. Often, these unique pieces of fabric end up being the ones you wish you could duplicate! Before you start painting make sure you have read the sections on fabric types, your work area, and safety tips on pages 12 and 13.

This is Jennifer's best example of "rejected" fabric. She painted a piece of green fabric and didn't like the outcome, so she put it in a trash bag and left it under her worktable for three months. Pulling it out later, she realized it was striking. What she might have thrown away eventually turned out to be a tremendous success story. The long curing time and excess water created a light, stunning piece of fabric with intricate, interwoven spider veins. It now decorates a wall in her office, as a reminder that a "swan lurks in every ugly duckling."

TIP
If the paint is highly diluted with water, the fabric might dry leaving spider veins. By working with wet or dry fabrics and in different weather conditions, you will achieve many varied results. Remember, there is no such thing as an unwanted or ugly piece of fabric!

Types of Paint

There are several types of fabric paint currently available. The most common types used by fiber artists are transparent, opaque, and metallic.

Transparent

Transparent paint is the favorite paint used by fiber artists; you will see it used in many of the fabric examples in this book. Brand names we recommend are Jacquard Dye-Na-Flow™ and Textile™ (semi-transparent), Pebeo Setacolor™ and Setasilk™, and PROchem PRO®Fab Textile semi-transparent paint. When properly diluted, transparent paints blend together easily, creating a "watercolor" effect. The paints can also blend together to create a second color; for example, painting blue over wet yellow creates green. Transparent paints leave the fabric with a soft "hand," similar to dyes.

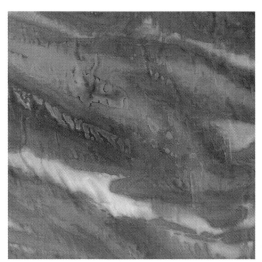

When painting one transparent color on top of another, you might wind up with a third color. This photo demonstrates how we painted yellow over wet blue to achieve green. The results, however, may be different if the bottom color has already dried.

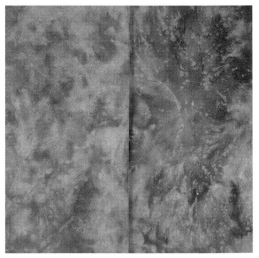

Even though paint particles sit on top of the fabric fibers, often both sides of the fabric can be used. The piece on the left is the reverse side of the piece on the right.

Opaque

Opaque paint is solid and dense with a paste-like consistency. The colors are bold and true, and they do not easily blend with surrounding colors. Opaque paint has a slightly thicker feel, or hand, on fabric than transparent paint. Brand names we recommend are Jacquard Neopaque™, Pebeo Setacolor Opaque™, PRO®Fab Opaque, and Jacquard Textile Paint™ (semi-opaque).

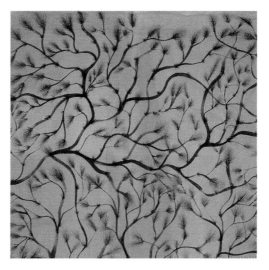

When painting motifs on fabric use opaque paints, and be sure you allow the paint to dry between colors.

Metallic

Metallic paint is perfect for highlighting or creating special effects, such as sunrays, water, or lightning. Although there is nothing more striking then the sparkle of metallic paints, use them sparingly, or as an accent, because they add a stiff hand to the fabric. To give your transparent paints a sparkle, mix them with 10 percent metallic paint, or over-paint the transparent paint with metallic paint that has been diluted 50 percent with water. Brand names we recommend are Jacquard Lumiere™, Pebeo Pearlescent™, PRO Chem PRObrite Pearlescent™, Jacquard Starbrite™, and Jacquard Pearl-Ex Pigments™.

Carole Fuller is a talented painter who created the delightful pieces shown above by painting a solid background color with diluted Pebeo Setacolor paint. Once the background dried, she painted on the stems, leaves, and flowers with tiny (#2 to #10) artist brushes, using undiluted opaque paints. Allow the paint to dry between colors.

Mixing metallic paint over transparent paint.

Blue Jacket, 2001, by Cindy Walter. Cindy created this exciting jacket by using The Tablecloth Shirt pattern by Lorraine Torrence Designs. After painting the fabric with various shades of blue Dye-Na-Flow paint, she over-painted it with a shear layer of silver Lumiere. For more information on Lorraine's patterns visit her website at www.lorrainetorrence.com.

For ideas on painting skies, nature scenes, and other motifs, refer to the "how-to" photos in watercolor painting books.

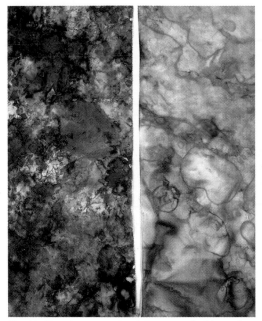

Dye-Na-Flow transparent paint was applied to a piece of dry silk habotai on the left and to a piece of wet silk on the right. You can see the amazing differences in the two results.

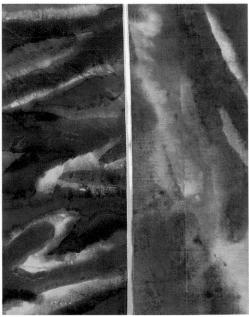

Setacolor transparent paint was applied to a piece of dry cotton on the left and a piece of wet cotton on the right. You can clearly see the pastel watercolor effect wet fabric produced, while bolder colors were achieved on dry fabric.

Basic Painting Information and Techniques

The basic painting techniques are very simple with only a few variances in application methods. Even if you are using the exact same colors of paint, the different applications will give you strikingly different results. Remember that working with wet or dry fabric, and the curing time, will alter the outcome. Choose the application technique that best suits your desired results.

After you learn to paint with transparent colors, experiment with other types of paints. Metallic and opaque paints can really "spark up" your project. Jennifer enjoys using metallic paints to highlight motifs in fabric, such as clouds and water. Try brushing a very light coat of metallic paint over the surface of the project.

Getting Started

For us, painting fabric is a way to relax. Remember to set an enjoyable mood in your workroom with music, flowers, fresh air, and any other pleasant stimulants. Let your mood, or the music, dictate your brush strokes and the colors you select. (**Note:** We suggest that you select two or three colors of paint for your first project.) Do not worry about the results; just have fun! Paint without any specific goal in mind, and let the colors and your creative expressions flow naturally.

Try taking commercially printed fabric and changing it to create a matching piece of fabric to add to your quilt or other project. Cindy designed the commercial print at top for Quilter's Only of Springs Industries. After washing the fabric in Synthrapol, she painted over it with transparent paints.

Jennifer finds that pieces of fabric she paints the first thing in the morning often match the colors she saw on the way to her studio, or the mood she felt when she woke up. She still warms up with a "mood" piece even if she has specific pieces she needs to paint for clients.

You will be diluting transparent paints with water to make them easier to spread and less stiff on the fabric. Most manufacturers recommend 25 to 50 percent paint dilution with water. We dilute Dye-Na-Flow by 25 percent, and Setacolor, Jacquard Textile, and PROfab Semi-transparent by 50 percent. If you want a lighter paint color, dilute it even more. Non-diluted paint will create a darker color, but it will also produce a rubbery or stiff fabric. Over-diluted paint will produce fabric with uneven coloring. Try it—you might love the results!

Before you start painting, you must decide if you want to work on wet or dry fabric; each produces a shockingly different result. If you want bold, rich colors, paint on dry fabric; however, if you want more of a watercolor effect, paint on wet fabric. Also, wet fabric allows the paint to blend easier, and the fabric will be much lighter in color once it has dried.

To paint on wet fabric, you should first mist the entire piece of fabric with water from a squirt bottle, or paint it with water using a large foam brush. Notice how we painted similar designs with the same paints on the fabrics on the top of page 40; the only difference is one was painted on wet fabric, the other on dry.

Mixing paint colors can be a fascinating experience. Study the color triangle on page 9, then experiment. Remember, if you use transparent paints, two colors applied on top of each other, or touching, will blend to create a third color (for example, if you paint a streak of yellow next to a streak of blue, green will appear between the blue and yellow where the paints overlap). If you do not want colors to blend, use an opaque paint, or thicken the transparent paint with a product, such as Jacquard's No-Flow or Pebeo Thickener.

If you are working on a project where the color needs to be consistent, consider using a manufactured color. If you choose to mix colors, write down the exact proportions of paint you mix together so you are able to re-create the color.

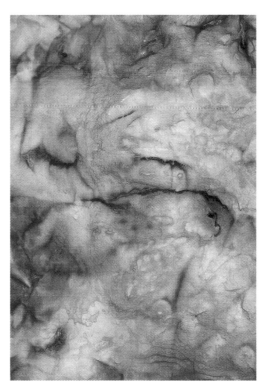

If you over-dilute paint there will not be enough paint particles suspended properly in the paint solution; however, if you "break the rules," you might achieve an unexpectedly pleasing "spidery pattern." Keep in mind, though, that paint contains an anti-bacterial agent that loses its effectiveness after being diluted with water. Don't save diluted paint for more than a few days.

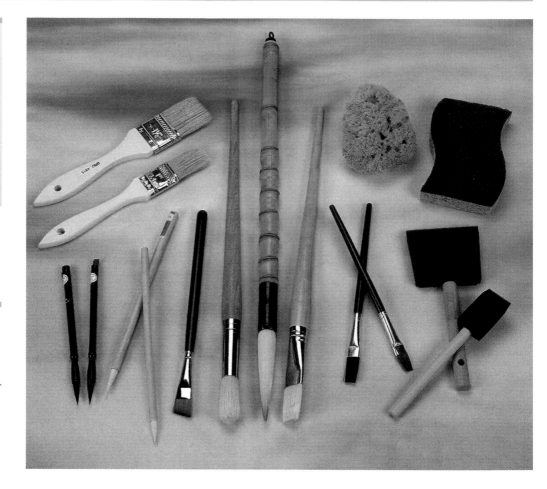

Brush Tips

Thoroughly clean brushes after each use by rinsing them in warm water. Do not leave them soaking in water for extended periods of time, especially Chinese bamboo brushes, because water can loosen the glue that holds the bristles into the tip.

Fabric artists collect a wide variety of brushes and tools to use with different painting methods. Buy a variety of inexpensive foam and bristle brushes to get started. As you become more familiar with the feel of different brushes, splurge and buy a few expensive ones.

YOU WILL NEED

- PFD fabric
- Table, with plastic cover
- Thumbtacks, silk tacks, or tape
- Transparent, opaque, and metallic paints, any colors
- Water spray bottle to wet fabric
- Variety of brushes and other application tools (such as sponges and stamps)
- Pitcher of water to wash brushes
- Pitcher of water to dilute paints
- Multiple plastic containers (such as yogurt or deli counter containers)
- Plastic gloves
- Paper towels
- Stirrers (such as long plastic or wooden spoons)

Supplies Needed for Painting

Remember to cover your table with plastic by securing it with tape or tacks (depending on the quality of your table) and always wear gloves, as well as old clothing and shoes. Collect the general supplies listed at left and have them handy when you are ready to create your own masterpiece.

Fixing Paint

The binders in paint polymerize when heated and become a solid grid, which sticks to the fabric. To fix the paint, wait until the painted fabric has completely dried and then iron it for 20 seconds in each area with a hot iron on the front and back side, or tumble in a hot clothes dryer for 30 minutes. You can use a chemical called Airfix to fix the paint in areas you cannot easily reach with an iron, such as paint stamped onto a lampshade. Regardless of the products you use, always follow the manufacturer's instructions.

Basic Painting Techniques

You are now ready to get started. Try the brush strokes and application methods on the following pages. Experiment, relax, and enjoy yourself.

Step 4

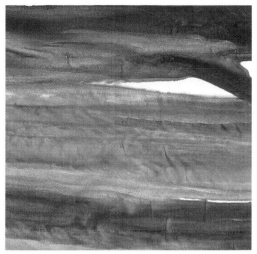
Step 5

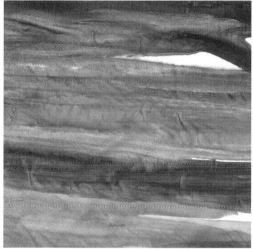
Step 6

The finished piece.

IMPORTANT
Paints appear darker when wet. To properly test the color you must paint a small piece of fabric and then let it dry to see if it is the color you desire.

Abstract Brush Stroke

Let's get started with a very basic painting technique by creating an abstract effect. For this sample, we applied the paint in long, sweeping brush strokes with a medium-sized foam brush. We selected purple, pink, golden yellow, and yellow for our colors. You can use these colors, or select three or four different transparent paints.

1 Tape or pin the PFD fabric to the plastic-covered table to secure.

2 Completely dampen the fabric by misting it with water from a squirt bottle, or by painting horizontal bands of water with a 3-inch foam brush.

3 Pour about a ⅛ cup of paint into a plastic container. Add ¹⁄₁₆ cup of water to dilute and thoroughly mix.

4 Start with the first color by making long, sweeping strokes on the fabric. Be sure to leave spaces of white so the next colors will have areas in which their hue will be pure and unmixed with the surrounding colors. You can vary the shade of the colors by adding more or less water to the paint mixture.

5 With sweeping strokes, add the next color. Because the fabric is wet, notice how the colors immediately start to blend to produce additional colors.

6 Once you are satisfied, stop! Remember, mixing too many colors can produce an unsatisfactory "muddy" color.

7 Allow the fabric to completely dry. Fix paint by thoroughly ironing on both sides of the fabric, or place in a clothes dryer for 30 minutes on high heat.

YOU WILL NEED
- Table, with plastic cover
- 1 yard PFD fabric
- Transparent paint, any colors
- Silk tacks or tape
- Water spray bottle to wet fabric
- Variety of brushes, including 3-inch foam
- Pitcher of water to wash brushes
- Pitcher of water to dilute paints
- Multiple plastic containers (such as yogurt or deli counter containers)
- Plastic gloves
- Paper towels

Step 3

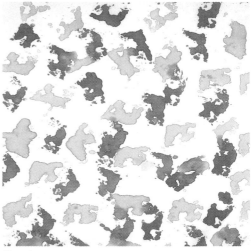

Step 4

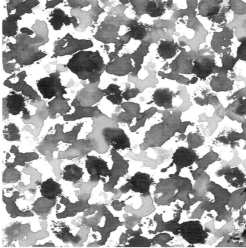

Step 5

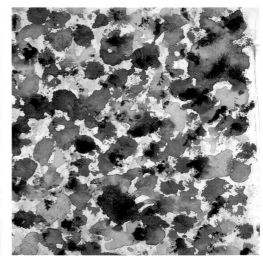

Step 6

YOU WILL NEED

- Table, with plastic cover
- 1 yard PFD fabric
- Thumbtacks, silk tacks, or tape
- Transparent paint, any color
- Metallic paint: Gold Lumiere
- Opaque paint: Black Neopaque
- Water spray bottle to wet fabric
- Sea sponge
- Pitcher of water to wash sponge
- Pitcher of water to dilute paints
- Multiple plastic containers (such as yogurt or deli counter containers)
- Plastic gloves
- Paper towels

Sponge Painting

Different sizes and types of sponges will create different effects. The outcome will vary depending on whether you use wet or dry fabric and the type of sponge. Sea sponges are great for dabbing texture onto fabric without creating a fully saturated look. Pick your paint colors, dilute, and start dabbing! In this project we used gold, brown, and black paint. We diluted all of the paints 50 percent with water, and diluted the black 90 percent to create gray. At the end we highlighted the fabric with dabs of metallic and opaque paint.

1 Tape or pin the PFD fabric to the plastic-covered table to secure.

2 Pour about ⅛ cup of the first paint into a plastic container and dilute with ¹⁄₁₆ cup of water.

3 Dab the sponge into the paint and then dab the sponge randomly on the fabric.

4 Randomly dab on the second color.

5 Continue dabbing the remaining colors onto the fabric.

6 As the final touch, add Jacquard gold Lumiere and black Neopaque paint. **Note:** These opaque and metallic paints sit on top of the translucent paints and add an exciting three-dimensional effect.

7 Allow the fabric to completely dry. Fix paint by thoroughly ironing on both sides of the fabric, or place in a clothes dryer for 30 minutes on high heat.

Step 4

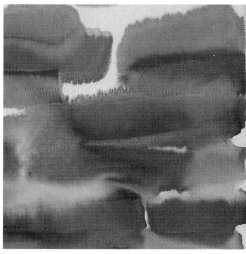

Step 5

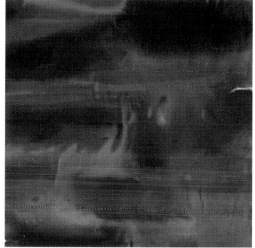

The finished piece.

Stubby Brush Strokes

The size and shape of your brush will create very different results. For this sample we used a wide 4-inch foam brush and made short, stubby strokes. We diluted sienna, black, and olive Dye-Na-Flow paints 50 percent with water.

1 Tape or pin the PFD fabric to the plastic-covered table to secure.

2 Completely dampen the fabric by misting it with water from a squirt bottle, or by painting horizontal bands of water with a 3-inch foam brush.

3 Pour about ⅛ cup of the first paint into a plastic container and dilute with ¹⁄₁₆ cup of water.

4 Add the first color using short stubby strokes.

5 Continue to add the remaining colors. **Note**: Because the fabric is wet, the colors mingle.

6 Allow the fabric to completely dry. Fix paint by thoroughly ironing on both sides of the fabric, or place in a clothes dryer for 30 minutes on high heat.

YOU WILL NEED
- 1 yard PFD fabric
- Table, with plastic cover
- Thumbtacks, silk tacks, or tape
- Transparent paint, any color
- Water spray bottle to wet fabric
- Variety of brushes, including 3- and 4-inch foam
- Pitcher of water to wash brushes
- Pitcher of water to dilute paints
- Multiple plastic containers (such as yogurt or deli counter containers)
- Plastic gloves
- Paper towels

The finished piece! We worked with wet fabric and diluted paints, so the resulting color is quite light. For darker or bolder colors, work with dry fabric. Note that the "peaks" of the scrunched folds will dry darker than the "valleys."

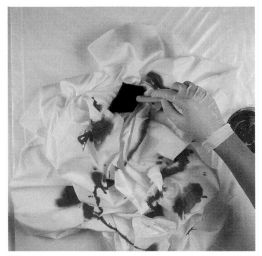

Step 3

Step 4

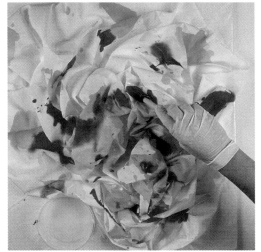

Step 5

Step 6

PROJECT IDEA

To make a scarf, simply roll-hem the PFD fabric prior to painting. We suggest using a 12- by 44-inch piece of silk.

YOU WILL NEED

- 1 PFD yard fabric
- Table, with plastic cover
- Transparent paint, any colors
- Water spray bottle to wet fabric
- 2-inch foam brush
- Pitcher of water to wash brush
- Pitcher of water to dilute paints
- Multiple plastic containers (such as yogurt or deli counter containers)
- Plastic gloves
- Paper towels

Scrunch Painting

We have found that the scrunch technique is one of the fastest and easiest methods to creatively paint fabric; it is a great way to use up your leftover paint, and is a lot of fun for children. The project must remain scrunched until it is dry, at least overnight. If you plan to use your work surface right away for something else, you can paint the fabric on a portable workspace, such as an old dishpan or large cookie sheet covered with plastic.

We used cotton fabric and four colors of paint (pink, green, yellow, and blue) for our sample, but choose any colors you desire.

1 Thoroughly dampen the PFD fabric. Scrunch it into a pile on top of your protected work surface.

2 Pour ⅛ cup of each paint into a separate container and dilute each with ¹⁄₁₆ cup of water.

3 Using the 2-inch foam brush, randomly place large drops of the first color around the scrunched fabric.

4 Repeat Step 3 for the second color.

5 Continue adding the remaining colors in the same manner.

6 Once you've added the last color, turn the fabric over and fill in any white areas on the other side. Allow the fabric to dry in this scrunched position.

7 **Optional:** To add more character to the fabric, re-scrunch or manipulate it several times while it is drying.

8 Allow the fabric to completely dry. Fix paint by thoroughly ironing on both sides of the fabric, or place in a clothes dryer for 30 minutes on high heat.

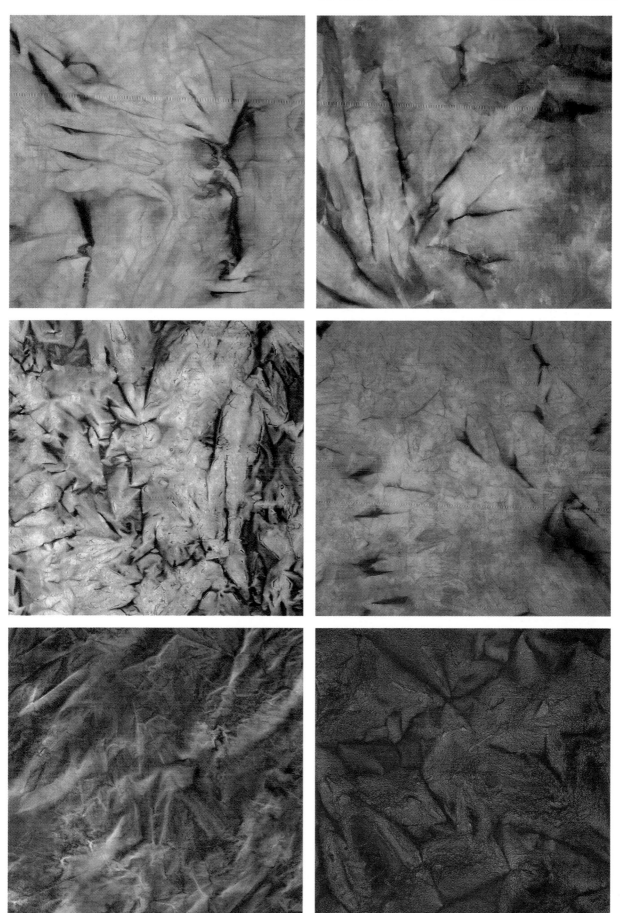

Other examples of scrunched fabrics.

TIP
This is a great technique for kids. For less mess, have them spray their fabric outside, right on the grass.

Step 3

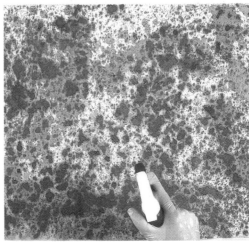
Step 4

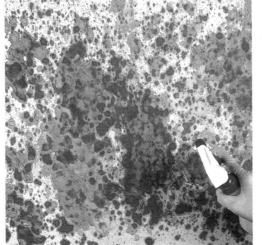
Step 5

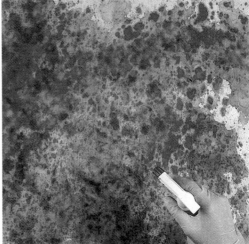
Step 6

PROJECT IDEA
Cindy liked the fabric so much in the different stages of these step-by-step photos that she decided to use them in the Painted Creation quilt on page 55.

YOU WILL NEED
- 1 yard PFD fabric
- Table, with plastic cover
- Thumbtacks, silk tacks, or tape
- Transparent paint, any color
- Spray bottles for paint (ideally one for each color)
- Pitcher of water to dilute paints in spray bottle
- Plastic gloves
- Paper towels
- Stirrer

Spray Bottle

What could be more fun or simple than applying paint from a spray bottle? This method works well on any fabric. Make sure you cover the floor area under your workspace with plastic, or work outside. We used green, pink, yellow, and blue in our project and worked with dry fabric, but you can also achieve a delightful effect with wet fabric.

1 Tape or pin the PFD fabric to the plastic-covered table to secure.

2 Select the color of paints you want to use. In separate mixing containers, dilute ⅛ cup of each paint with ¹⁄₁₆ cup of water; thoroughly mix.

3 Pour the first paint mixture into a spray bottle. Mist paint onto fabric. Do not let the paints dry between each color application.

4 Be sure to thoroughly rinse the bottle before filling it with next color. Spray the second color.

5 Continue spraying different colors of paint until you are satisfied with the results. Remember, too many colors can produce a disappointing "muddy" shade.

6 You can color all of the white spots with spray or even a foam brush, or let the white show through.

7 Allow the fabric to completely dry. Fix paint by thoroughly ironing on both sides of the fabric, or place in a clothes dryer for 30 minutes on high heat.

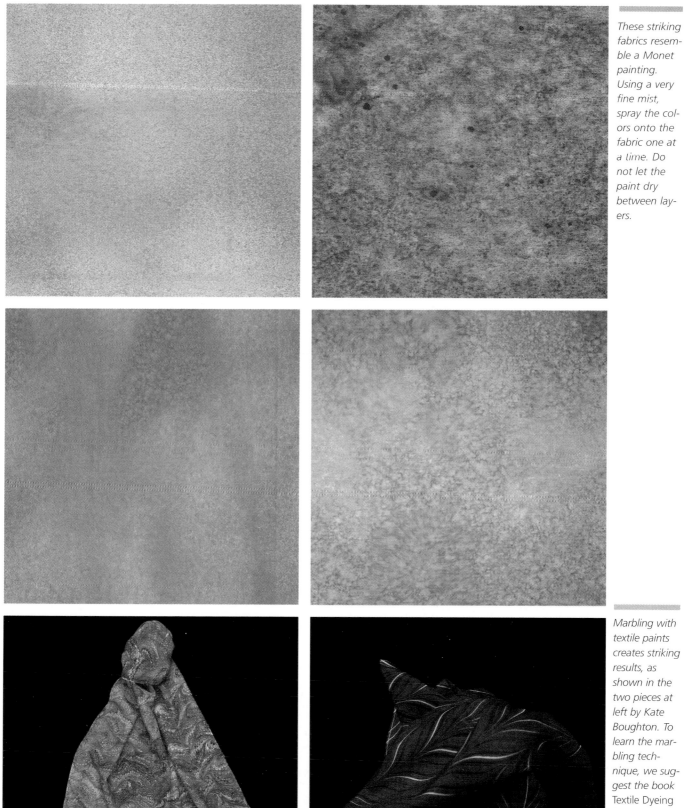

These striking fabrics resemble a Monet painting. Using a very fine mist, spray the colors onto the fabric one at a time. Do not let the paint dry between layers.

Marbling with textile paints creates striking results, as shown in the two pieces at left by Kate Boughton. To learn the marbling technique, we suggest the book Textile Dyeing (see Recommended Reading, page 94). Photos courtesy of Rupert, Gibbon & Spider, Inc.

Cindy created this charming fabric using large-grained rock salt, the old-fashioned kind of salt used for making ice cream; it is available at your local supermarket.

Diana Morrison created this elegant piece of fabric with small-grained salt from Jacquard.

SAVE AND REUSE SALT

After the fabric has dried, save the salt you have brushed off and store it for your next project.

YOU WILL NEED

- 1 yard PFD fabric
- Table, with plastic cover
- Thumbtacks, silk tacks, or tape
- Transparent paint, any color
- Sea or rock salt
- Water spray bottle to wet fabric
- Variety of brushes
- Pitcher of water to wash brushes
- Pitcher of water to dilute paints
- Multiple plastic containers (such as yogurt or deli counter containers)
- Plastic gloves
- Paper towels

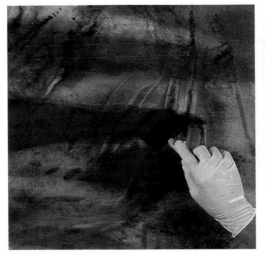

Step 2

Step 3

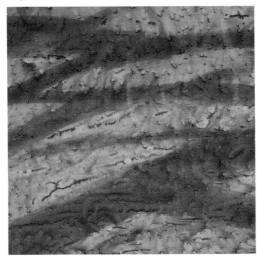

The finished piece, once dried.

We salted the top section of this fabric, but not the bottom. Isn't the difference remarkable?

Salted Fabric

Salting silk or cotton to achieve a starburst affect is truly one of our favorite methods to create a one-of-a-kind piece of fabric. We love to use sea salt and rock salt because their granules are larger than table salt, and the results are stunning.

1 Tape or pin the PFD fabric to the plastic-covered table to secure. Wet the fabric with a spray bottle or large brush strokes of water.

2 Paint an abstract design using your desired colors of transparent paint.

3 Sprinkle salt on the fabric, while the paint is still wet. **Note:** Once the painted fabric has dried, you cannot re-wet the paint and then apply salt. You will see the effect of the salt once the paint dries.

4 Allow the fabric to completely dry. Brush off the salt and save it for your next project.

5 Fix paint by thoroughly ironing on both sides of the fabric, or place in a clothes dryer for 30 minutes on high heat.

Painting on Silk With a Frame

Whenever you want to paint a specific motif on silk, it is necessary to stretch the fabric on a frame (just like when working with dyes; see page 26). Lines of gutta resist, a textile paint, are applied to this fabric to prevent the paints from bleeding together (see page 30). Try working with colored gutta for a stained-glass effect. Talented fiber artist Kim Meyer shares her instructions with us so you can create your own vest. For this project you will need your own vest pattern and designs that you want to paint onto the vest.

1 Cut out the paper pattern for the vest (top only, not the lining). Pin the pattern pieces to the silk.

2 Using a disappearing ink pen, trace the outline of the vest pattern onto the silk. Remove the pattern.

3 Using the same pen, draw guidelines for your design. Here, Kim drew sections of flower gardens. Because the silk is semi-transparent you could trace designs from a photo or drawing.

4 Pin silk tautly to the frame.

5 Trace the design lines made in Step 3 with black gutta resist. Allow to dry.

6 Paint and have fun! Mix and match the paint colors, following the design pattern of your choice.

7 When the design is finished, allow the paint to dry completely before removing the silk from the frame

8 Fix paint by thoroughly ironing on both sides of the fabric.

9 Cut out the remaining pattern pieces and sew the vest together, following pattern instructions.

YOU WILL NEED

- Vest pattern with a lining
- Fabric per pattern
- Designs to trace onto the silk
- Dye-Na-Flow paints, any colors
- Several medium round brushes
- Frame and silk tacks
- Gutta resist, black, with applicator bottle and #7 tip
- Disappearing ink pen
- Pitcher of water to wash brushes
- Pitcher of water to dilute paints
- Multiple plastic containers (such as yogurt or deli counter containers)
- Plastic gloves
- Paper towels

Step 3

YOU WILL NEED

- Table, with plastic cover
- Thumbtacks, silk tacks, or tape
- Pre-painted, or printed, PFD base fabric
- Metallic or opaque paint, any colors
- Variety of brushes, including 1-inch round
- Pitcher of water to wash brushes
- Pitcher of water to dilute paints
- Multiple plastic containers (such as yogurt or deli counter containers)
- Plastic gloves
- Paper towels

Over-painting

You can add paint on top of dried paint or commercially printed fabric to change the look of the fabric; this is called over-painting. Jennifer painted this striking piece of fabric with Pebeo Pearlescent metallic paint and a 1-inch round paintbrush.

1 Tape or pin the PFD base fabric to the plastic-covered table to secure.

2 If you are over-painting on a base color that you have painted, wait until it completely dries to over-paint your motifs.

3 Over-paint swirls or any motif with metallic or opaque paints.

4 Allow the fabric to completely dry. Fix paint by thoroughly ironing on both sides of the fabric, or place in a clothes dryer for 30 minutes on high heat.

For a subtle look, Cindy over-painted these motifs with mostly transparent paints and only a few metallic paints.

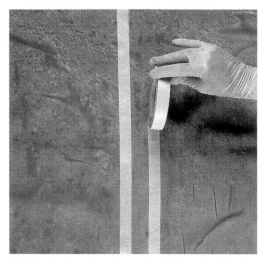

Step 2

Step 3

Step 4

The finished piece.

Painted Grid

YOU WILL NEED
- 1 yard PFD fabric
- Table, with plastic cover
- Thumbtacks, silk tacks, or tape
- Opaque and metallic paint, any colors
- Transparent paint for base, any color
- Medium-sized brush
- Masking tape (any width)
- Pitcher of water to wash brushes
- Multiple plastic containers (such as yogurt or deli counter containers)
- Plastic gloves
- Paper towels

For this form of over-painting, we used masking tape to divide the areas where we wanted to apply opaque (Neopaque) and metallic (Lumiere) paints on top of a base of transparent paint. Apply the masking tape in any pattern and then apply the paints undiluted so they don't bleed under the tape.

1 Tape or pin the PFD fabric to the plastic-covered table to secure. Paint the base color and let the fabric completely dry.

2 Place strips of masking tape on the fabric in any pattern. Here, we made a checkerboard.

3 Cindy and Jennifer painted alternating blocks, but you can create any pattern that appeals to you.

4 Dab opaque and metallic paints on in any pattern with a medium-sized brush.

5 Once the paint has completely dried, remove the tape.

6 Allow the fabric to completely dry. Fix paint by thoroughly ironing on both sides of the fabric, or place in a clothes dryer for 30 minutes on high heat.

Painted Creation, 40" x 40", 2001, by Cindy Walter. There are few accomplishments as rewarding as making a quilt entirely with fabrics you have created. Jennifer and Cindy painted these fabrics for the step-by-step photos in this book. After the "steps" were photographed, Cindy combined the fabrics into a memory quilt as a tribute to the book. Notice how she used the painted grid fabric as a focal point.

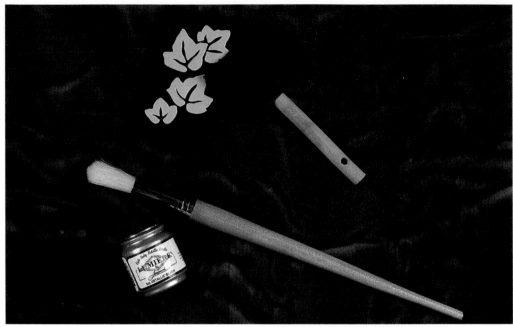

Basic supplies needed for stamping on fabric.

Step 3

Step 4

Stamping

Stamping paint is a perfect way to apply a "motif" on your fabric. It is a fun technique, even for children. You can purchase stamps of endless motifs at any craft store, or create your own by cutting out pieces of Styrofoam or sponge.

1 Tape or pin the PFD fabric to the plastic-covered table to secure.

2 You can stamp onto any color of fabric. For this project, we first painted the base black with transparent paint and a 3-inch foam brush. Let the base paint dry.

3 Paint the accent color on the stamp with a medium-sized brush. We selected silver metallic Lumiere as our accent color.

4 Press the stamp on the fabric in a random pattern until you achieve the desired affect.

5 Allow the fabric to completely dry. Fix paint by thoroughly ironing on both sides of the fabric, or place in a clothes dryer for 30 minutes on high heat.

YOU WILL NEED
- 1 yard PFD fabric
- Table, with plastic cover
- Thumbtacks, silk tacks, or tape
- Transparent, opaque, or metallic paint, any colors
- Transparent paint for base, any color
- Variety of stamps
- 3-inch foam brush and medium-sized bristle brush
- Multiple plastic containers (such as yogurt or deli counter containers)
- Plastic gloves
- Paper towels

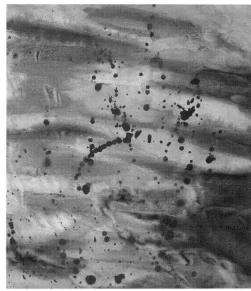

We thought the splatter ruined the piece...

but we just added more!

Splatter Painting

The results you get with splatter painting are a little unpredictable, but it sure can be a lot of fun! We suggest using this method outside.

Here, we used a piece of fabric we painted in the abstract method with a brush. Red paint accidentally splattered on the fabric. Our first thought was that the piece was ruined, but we decided to add more splatters of red paint and thus created a fabulous piece of fabric.

1 Tape or pin the pre-painted PFD fabric to the plastic-covered table to secure.

2 Dab your brush into the paint and simply shake the brush above the fabric to "splatter" it in a random pattern.

3 Allow the fabric to completely dry. Fix paint by thoroughly ironing on both sides of the fabric, or place in a clothes dryer for 30 minutes on high heat.

SPLATTER PAINTING IS EASY
Mary Reeves of the Bernina Sewing Center in Greenville, South Carolina, says in her thick southern drawl, "Whether you splatter, spray, or dab, paintin' fabric is as easy as fallin' off a log."

YOU WILL NEED
- 1 yard PFD fabric, pre-painted
- Table, with plastic cover
- Thumbtacks, silk tacks, or tape
- Transparent, opaque, or metallic paint, any colors
- Variety of brushes and other application tools
- Pitcher of water to wash brushes
- Pitcher of water to dilute paints
- Multiple plastic containers (such as yogurt or deli counter containers)
- Plastic gloves
- Paper towels

Jane Varcoe created these beautiful pieces of fabric by first painting abstract lines, and then splattering over the original design with gold paint.

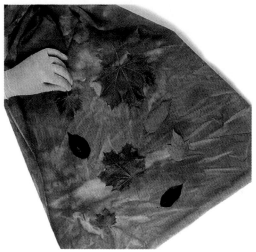

Step 3

The finished piece.

YOU WILL NEED

- 1 yard PFD fabric
- Table, with plastic cover
- Thumbtacks, silk tacks, or tape
- Objects, such as leaves, flowers, rice, or cutouts
- Transparent paints, any color
- Water spray bottle to wet fabric
- Variety of brushes and other application tools
- Pitcher of water to wash brushes
- Pitcher of water to dilute paints
- Multiple plastic containers (such as old yogurt or deli counter containers)
- Plastic gloves
- Paper towels

Heliographic

Heliographic art is an ancient technique in which images are used to make an impression, or sunprint, on the fabric. We used leaves in our sample, but you can also try flowers, long-grain rice, pinecones, or even cardboard cutouts. You must use transparent paint for this process. We've had great success with Jacquard Textile Paint, Pebeo Setacolor, and Dye-Na-Flow. Use your imagination to come up with other ways to achieve new and interesting results.

Placing the fabric in the hot sun with the images on top is how traditional heliographic images were created. We've discovered that a heat lamp, or bright light, will also do the trick. The area under the image takes longer to cure because it is covered, resulting in a lighter area, or impression, on the fabric. You must place the objects on the fabric right away, while the paint is wet.

Once your fabric has been painted and dried, you cannot re-wet it to create a heliographic image.

1 Tape or pin the PFD fabric to the plastic-covered table to secure. Wet the fabric with a spray bottle or large brush strokes of water.

2 Paint any color in any pattern on the fabric with transparent paint.

3 Place the objects on top of the freshly painted, wet fabric. The objects must be placed firmly against the fabric with no air pockets.

4 Place the fabric in the hot sun, or under a very bright light, to dry.

5 Allow the fabric to completely dry. Fix paint by thoroughly ironing on both sides of the fabric, or place in a clothes dryer for 30 minutes on high heat.

Jennifer's mother, Jane, always creates her heliographic prints outside on the grass without a table. She created these beautiful pieces with a variety of leaves.

Additional Color Inspiration

The following pages show you additional color combinations, most in a step-by-step format, to create fabric with themes or for certain projects. We painted most of these fabrics with long, abstract strokes to show you how easy it is to combine colors.

A wide array of dyed and painted fabrics. The colors shown are just a sampling of what you can achieve.

Green Forest

   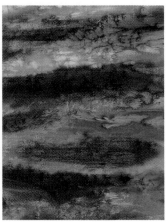

We first combined green and yellow paints, then ended with streaks of purple. Note that purple and yellow make brown, which is a tertiary color (purple is made from red and blue, and combining it with yellow uses all three primary colors). To give the fabric additional character, we sprinkled salt on top of the paint before it dried (see page 50).

Garden

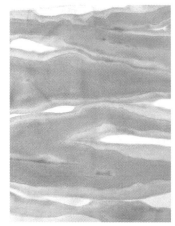  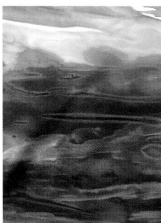 

Here, we started by painting strokes of light and medium greens, then added touches of pink and burgundy. Note that blending green with pink or red tones will create a shade of brown (because it now becomes a tertiary color and contains all three primary colors). If you want bright areas of pink or other "flower" colors, leave white areas on the fabric when you are painting the green.

Sunset

   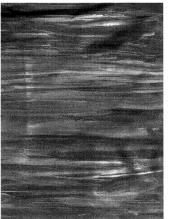

We started this fabric with streaks of fuchsia and blue paints. Note that red and blue make purple, so in the areas where the two colors overlap it created a third color. We highlighted the fabric with bands of gold Lumiere.

Pink Sherbet

   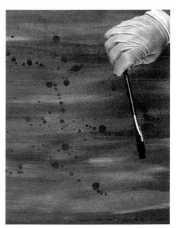

We started this fabric by painting it with a solid layer of pink. We added streaks of orange but felt it didn't show enough, so we added streaks of yellow to create a brighter color (red and yellow create orange). We then added a shear layer of silver Lumiere. To give the fabric additional character, try the splatter technique on page 57.

Garnet

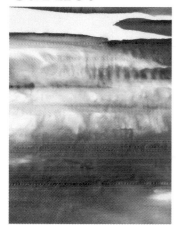   

Here, we started with rose, yellowish rust, and then added blue. The blue will turn green when mixed with the yellowish rust, so leave white areas where the blue can shine through (see the last photo). We topped this fabric off with a thin layer of gold Lumiere.

Earth Tones

   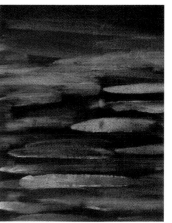

We started this piece with streaks of burgundy, then added brown and a darker brown. If you want to paint dark, rich soil, stop there. We went a step further, though, and added streaks of gold and bronze Lumiere.

Overcast Sky

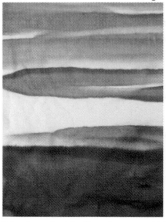  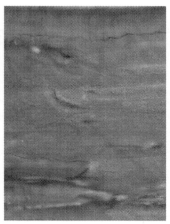 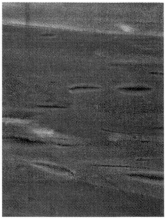

We started with diluted gray and black paints, then added streaks of blue. We then topped our piece with streaks of silver Lumiere. In the last photo see how we repeated the process, this time with our paints more concentrated so that ending result was darker.

Simply Playing

 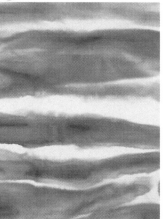 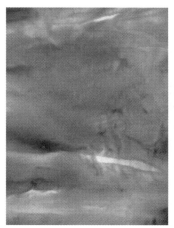 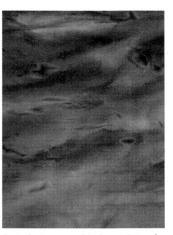

Here, we used streaks of diluted blue paint to show you three great ways to create clouds for sky fabric. In the last photo, we added a variety of colors to all of the white areas to create a stunning multi-hued piece of fabric that you can use in any type of project.

Desert Sunset

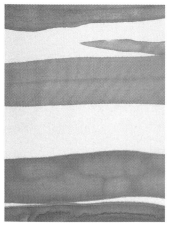   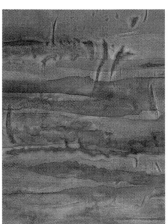

We started with large streaks of teal and then added streaks of golden yellow in the white areas. Note in the second photo where the golden yellow is painted over the teal it creates a soft green, while in the next photo where the yellow is painted on a white area, the color is purer. We added very small streaks of red at the end of the process.

Desert

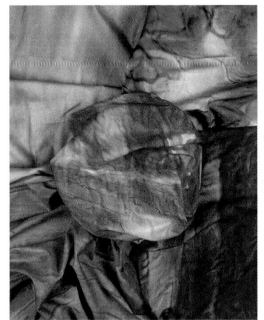

Purples

Pastels

Beautiful Skies

Perfect Sky

Dawn

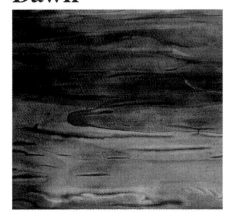

Bright Opal

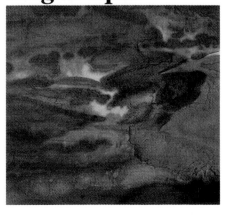

Projects Created With Dyed & Painted Fabrics

Chamber Series, 16" x 20",
2000, by Melody Johnson.
Melody painted the cotton
and cotton muslin fabrics
used in this beautiful quilt
(which is one of a series of
five quilts) with a large
variety of mediums, including acrylic paint, ink,
Pebeo Setacolor, colored
pencils, watercolor
crayons, and gel pens. In
addition to the cotton fabric, she also used dyed
cheesecloth. To view more
of her remarkable quilts
visit her website at
www.artfabrik.com.

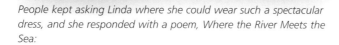

People kept asking Linda where she could wear such a spectacular dress, and she responded with a poem, Where the River Meets the Sea:

I'm searching for a place where the river meets the sea,
Where crashing crystal waterfalls meet their destiny,
Where waves with wild abandon advance upon the shore
With silken waves and shining foam and then retreat once more.
And one day, when I find that place, I'll dance among them there,
All in my fancy sea foam dress, with ribbons in my hair;
With crystal beads around my neck, I'll dance beneath the moon,
And THAT is where I'll wear this dress—I'm sure I'll find it soon.

Where the River Meets the Sea, 1999, by Linda Schmidt. Linda created this remarkable garment ensemble for the 1997-98 Fairfield Fashion Show. The dress is constructed with dissolvable Sulky Solvy and more than 17,000 yards of thread. It is layered over another dress of silk, which was hand-dyed with Jacquard Silk Colors. She dyed white fabric pumps and a purse at the same time with the same dyes. The jacket is constructed from a combination of fabrics by Fabrics To Dye For, Skydyes, Cherrywood Fabrics, and Thai Silk. To view more of Linda's incredible work visit her website at http://shortattn.home.attbi.com.

Sun Dancer, 50" x 40", 1998, by Deborah Sylvester and Cindy Walter. Debra started this striking quilt in a Snippet workshop taught by Cindy at the International Quilt Festival in Houston, Texas, on a piece of tie-dyed cotton. Her talent as a fiber artist shines with her excellent choice of colors. Cindy added additional motion with the machine quilting lines and couched-on yarns. The quilt has won several awards and is featured in More Snippet Sensations. *For more information on tie-dyeing and Shibori techniques, we recommend the book* Shibori *(see Recommended Reading, page 94).*

Gala Gold for the New Millennium, 1999, by Peggy True. This original design features large appliqués edged with gold satin stitch, couched trims, machine embroidery, machine quilting, and painted cotton fabric from Fabrics To Dye For. *For more information refer to the book* True Style *in the Recommended Reading section (page 94), or contact her at TruWay@aol.com.*

Blossoms in the Mist, 1999, by Peggy True. Peggy used her distinctive appliqué and piecing methods to create this jacket featuring Fabrics To Dye For painted cotton fabric. For more information refer to the book True Style *in the Recommended Reading section (page 94), or contact her at TruWay@aol.com.*

Hummin' Glory, 28" x 30", 2001, by Maria Lage. Maria's love of nature provides her with the inspiration for many of her original appliqué designs. Hand-dyed and -painted fabrics give her an unlimited palette of fabric to capture nature in all of its glory. Jennifer painted the "Monet" fabric used for the background.

Lady of the Lake, 40" x 46", 1999, by Linda Schmidt. Linda started this original design with a group of painted fabric from Fabrics To Dye For and the desire to make a little boy in a deep rocky, forest. During a class taught by Joan Colvin, her original plans went to the wayside, and the trees and water became a tropical beach, not a deep forest. The lady was added last to resemble Jennifer and her mother, Jane Varcoe.

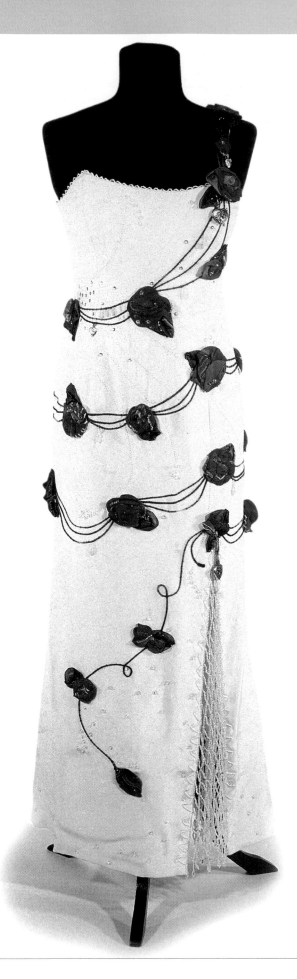

Rose Remembrance to Pai & Sogra, 2000, by Anna Mazur. This beautiful ensemble was featured in the 2000 Fairfield Fashion Show, and is dedicated to the memory of Anna's father and mother-in-law who lost their lives to cancer while she was creating it. The strapless gown is an adaptation of Vogue Pattern #2237 and made from four-ply silk with an underlining of two layers of silk organza and a layer of silk crepe de chine. The layers of silk create a foundation to support the three-dimensional garland of roses and floral vines created by silk satin, which Jennifer custom painted. The gown and purse are embellished with Swarovski Austrian crystals, beads, and charms.

Dragonfly Meadow, 35" x 35", 2001, by Susan E. Stedman. Susan pieced the background together first. Then she created the three-dimensional dragonflies by sewing two layers together, turning them right-side out, and then tacking them down so they remained free-standing. The use of hand-painted fabrics from Fabrics To Dye For in this commercial pattern from Java House Quilts makes this a very special quilt.

Moon Phases II, 32" x 22", 1999, by Laura Cater-Woods. Quilts created by this award-winning fiber artist have been exhibited in shows and galleries across the United States. Her ribbons and awards are too numerous to list! For this quilt, Laura used fabrics painted primarily by Jane Varcoe, with a few commercial fabrics. To view more of her remarkable quilts visit her website at www.artquilter.net.

Cindy has had the pleasure of teaching in New Zealand several times. She loves collecting fabrics from her "Kiwi" friends. These beautiful fabrics were created by Material Arts New Zealand. The base color is dyed and then over-painted with transparent and opaque paints. For more information, visit their website at www.materialartsnz.com.

Echo/Fragment #4, 2001, by Laura Cater-Woods. Laura is fascinated by the patterns of time created in nature. This quilt began with the lines found on driftwood, shells, rocks, and objects from the garden. Working with fabric and stitched surfaces illustrates that art is a verb by which we reveal our world to others and ourselves. This talented fiber artist created the quilt with painted cottons from Fabrics To Dye For. To view more of her remarkable quilts visit her website at www.artquilter.net.

A Rainbow Swirl, 49" x 49", 1998, by Stacy Michell. Stacy dyed the fabric, Marti Michell designed the top using Perfect Patchwork templates, Toni Hearn pieced the top, and Cindy Walter hand-quilted it. The beautiful fabrics used in this quilt merge together the Martha Washington and Rambler blocks to create a striking pattern. This quilt is featured in Cindy and Diana Leone's book, Fine Hand Quilting.

Stacy Michell, owner of Shades Textiles, dyed these 100-percent cottons using the immersion technique. To view more of her beautiful fabrics visit her website at www.shadestextiles.com.

Life is Just a Bowl of Cherries, 60" x 45", 2000, by Barbara Barrick McKie. This quilt was selected for Fiber Directions 2001 and won Best in USA at the World Quilt Show in 2001. Barbara created all of the fabrics in this project. This piece represents a complex number of surface design techniques, including immersion dyed cotton, dye-painted cotton, hand-painted disperse-dyed polyester, and disperse-dyed polyester photo transfers. The piece is machine appliquéd, pieced, and quilted. Visit www.sublimation.com for more information on Disperse Dye Inks. Visit Barbara's website at www.mckieart.com to view more of her remarkable work.

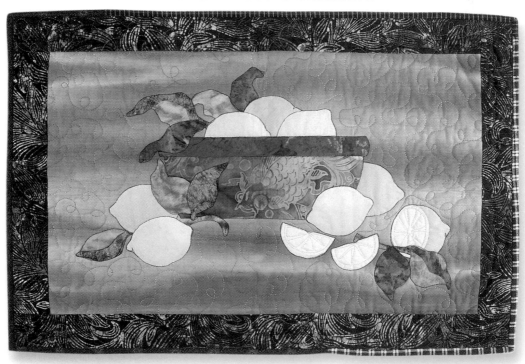

Lemon Bowl, 21" x 36", 1998, by Beth Polouski. Beth created this zesty wall hanging with fabrics from Fabrics To Dye For and her original pattern. The pattern is available from Fabrics To Dye For.

Montana, 26" x 30", 1997, by Cindy Walter. Cindy has always been attracted to beautiful fabric, and this quilt is full of hand-dyed fabrics she has collected over the years. She used one of her all-time-favorite fabrics as a focal point in the sky; Mickey Lawyer, the author of Skydyes, painted the fabric. We recommend her book because she has an impressive painting style, and the book is full of beautiful projects. For more information visit her website at www.skydyes.com.

Reversible Vest, 2001, by Dwen Heminway. Garments are a great way to use painted fabrics. Dwen used the Madame Butterfly pattern in Carol Doak's book, Easy Reversible Vests. Jennifer painted the silk lining using a Shibori technique. Jennifer and her mother, Jane, painted the fabrics used for the outside of the vest.

Carschenna, 44" x 88", 2000, by Barbara Malanowski. Barbara lives in a tiny village high in the Swiss Alps. Her inspiration for many of her quilts comes from the beauty that surrounds her home. This quilt is an adaptation of pre-historical symbols from around 10,000-5,000 BC on stones found near her home region. She hand-painted silk with Dupont paints and then embellished the quilt with machine quilting.

Betty Ricketts created the picture on this T-shirt with Dye-Na-Flow and black gutta resist. Photo courtesy of Rupert, Gibbon & Spider, Inc.

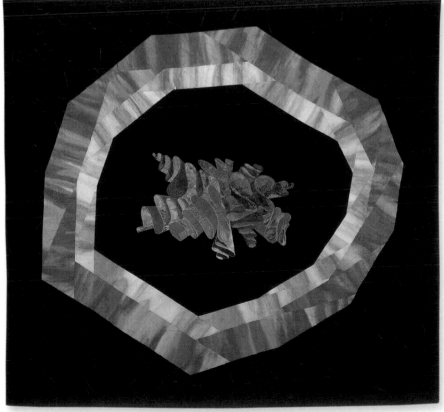

Ribbons Exploding, 72" x 72", 2001, by Cara Gulati. The effect of the ribbons expanding from the center of this remarkable quilt was achieved with the placement of fabric, as well as the thread color and textured quilting. Cara used both painted and dyed fabrics in this quilt.

Feather Study #1, 78" x 65", 1999, by Caryl Bryer Fallert. A macro photograph of a Guinea fowl feather inspired this world-famous fiber artist to design this quilt, which is made of hand-dyed fabrics. Caryl first experimented with the design on the computer using values of black, white, and gray and then added color to the computer image. Visit her website at www.bryerpatch.com to view more of her quilts.

Feather Study #11, 48" x 48", 2000, by Caryl Bryer Fallert. This is one in a series of quilts Caryl created that was inspired by the close-up view of a feather, which evolved from hundreds of drawings on this theme. The color gradation of hand-dyed fabrics creates the illusion of light in this quilt. Visit her website at www.bryerpatch.com to view more of her quilts.

Midnight Fantasy #2, 48" x 48", 2000, by Caryl Bryer Fallert. The design for this quilt came to Caryl during a sleepless night when she got out of bed and made a series of small drawings to pass the time. She created the swirling effect on this dynamic quilt with hand-dyed fabrics. Visit her website at www.bryerpatch.com to view more of her quilts.

Aquarium #1: Fish Tails, 60" x 44", 2001, by Caryl Bryer Fallert. This quilt began as a small sketch Caryl made after returning from the Great Barrier Reef in Australia. She kept the sketch for 13 years and didn't actually start the quilt until after a snorkeling trip to Kauai. The fabrics were hand-dyed and -painted in variegated gradations to create the soft focus effects of an underwater scene. The quilting was done with many different colors of polyester thread. Visit her website at www.bryerpatch.com to view more of her quilts.

Tranquility in Purple, 50" x 51", 2001, by Cindy Walter. Cindy feels we should give back to our communities through our creative passions. She created this piece of wall art as a donation to a very special charity called Giant Steps Therapeutic Equestrian Center, a nonprofit organization dedicated to improving the quality of life for individuals with physical, emotional, and developmental disabilities. The quilt top is constructed exclusively from fabric she and Jennifer painted, while the fabrics on the back of the quilt are prints Cindy designed for Springs Industries. The quilt is embellished with a variety of thread designs in each block. In the private collection of Tony and Nancy Lilly.

Painted Petals, 51" x 52", 2001, by Joan Shay. Joan created this original design with Fabrics To Dye For fabric painted by Jennifer and her mother, Jane, and her own unique Petal Play patterns. Kits, including the fabric and patterns, are available as a block of the month project from Fabrics To Dye For and Petal Play. It was appliquéd by Joan and quilted by Judy Irish. To view more blocks from Petal Play visit www.PetalPlay.com. Photograph by Warren Roos.

Sunset in the Japanese Garden, 45" x 45", 2000, by Louisa L. Smith. This quilt was the tenth in a series of quilts that Louisa designed using her Strips 'n Curves method. The traditional Japanese graphic designs raked in sand gardens inspired the name of this quilt. She used a combination of hand-painted fabrics from Fabrics To Dye For and commercial fabrics from David Textiles, Inc. The pattern for this quilt can be found in her book, Strips 'n Curves.

Sunflowers II, 65¹/₂" x 48¹/₂", 2001, by Melody Johnson. Melody created the cotton fabrics in this quilt using Procion MX dyes and the direct application. To view more of her incredible quilts visit her website at www.artfabrik.com.

Hand-woven Rug, 30" x 40", and Purse, 2001, by Janney M. Simpson. Hand-painted fabrics are perfect to use in home décor objects. This talented fiber artist made this woven rug and purse on a four-shaft floor loom with a plain weave pattern, cotton carpet warp, and fabric from Fabrics To Dye For. For custom weaving or information on weaving classes contact Janney at Janney416@aol.com.

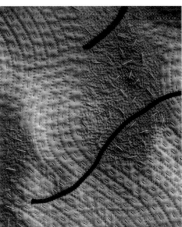

False Impression, 58" x 42", 1997, by Barbara Oliver Hartman. Barbara began this quilt with a piece of hand-dyed cotton sateen as the background. The surface design elements were added with appliqué and reverse appliqué. This award-winning quilt has been featured in numerous quilt shows and is included in Cindy and Diana Leone's book, Fine Hand Quilting. *Photograph by Barbara Oliver Hartman.*

Projects

We wanted to give you some extra projects, beyond those presented in Sections 2 and 3. Here, you will find a pillow, two quilts (each with full-size patterns), and a cover-up, all of which incorporate painted and dyed fabrics.

PROJECT 1
Merryflower Pillow

Merryflower Pillow, 16" x 16", 2001, by Lynn LaBelle. A great and easy way to incorporate hand-painted or -dyed fabrics into your décor is with pillows.

YOU WILL NEED

- Fabrics
  - 15 strips of painted fabric, 20" long x 1" to 3" widths, in varying colors
  - Backing, 2 pieces 15" x 22", any color
  - Trim, 2 pieces 3" x 18" and 2 pieces 3" x 23", any color
- Basic machine sewing supplies
- Rotary cutting equipment
- 16" x 16" pillow form

1 Sew the long edges of the strips of fabric together. Iron the seams to one side. Trim this "strata" section to 18 x 18 inches to create the pillow top.

2 Sew the two shorter trim pieces to the sides of the pillow top. Sew the two longer pieces to the top and bottom of the pillow top. Iron the seams toward the center of the top.

3 To create the pillow back, press one of the long 22-inch edges under 2 inches to create a 2-inch hem. Top stitch. Repeat for the other back piece.

4 With right sides together, line up the raw edges of the pillow top with the two back pieces, putting the hemmed area to the center. The hemmed areas will overlap to create the opening in which you will insert the pillow form. Using a ⅝-inch seam allowance, stitch the back pieces to the top.

5 Turn right side out and press flat.

6 Carefully stitch around all four sides in the seam line between the strata strips and the trim.

7 Insert pillow form.

PROJECT 2
Sunrise, Sunset Quilt

Sunrise, Sunset, 46" x 50", 1998, by Barbara W. Barber. This lonely heron, illuminated by dawn, peers longingly into the distance as if gazing at her feathered friends in flight. Barbara made this quilt with fabrics painted by Jane Varcoe. Create this pattern using the appliqué method of your choice. If you plan to use a raw-edge technique, use the patterns as they are. If you plan to use a basted under edge technique, add ⅜ inch when cutting out each pattern.

1 Paint the sky and water pieces with horizontal strokes to create a mirror effect.

2 Appliqué the mountains to the bottom edge of the sky fabric.

3 Sew the sky and ground fabric together to create the foundation.

4 Copy the heron pattern from the enclosed pattern sheet. Use this as your template to cut out the heron.

5 For the placement guide, pin the body of the heron to the foundation. Then tuck the neck, feathers, and legs under the body. Appliqué the entire heron to the foundation.

6 You are now ready to add the borders. **Note:** Lamé is used for the inner border. Sew the smaller border strips to the sides. Sew on the top and bottom strip.

7 Layer the backing, batting, and top. Baste using your preferred method.

8 Free motion machine-quilt or hand-embroider the flying birds in the sky. Then machine quilt the rest of the project in a free-flowing design, following the streaks of color in the foundation fabric and the shapes of the heron's body. Add "puddle" circles around its feet.

9 Bind.

YOU WILL NEED
- Heron pattern
- Fabrics
  - ½ yard for sky
  - ½ yard for water
  - Assorted scraps for mountains
  - Assorted scraps for heron
  - ½ yard lame
  - 1½ yard for border
  - 3¼ yard for backing
- Cotton batting cut 48" x 52"
- Appliqué supplies
- Machine sewing and quilting supplies

PROJECT 3
Sun Showers Quilt

Sun Showers, 24" x 20", 1997, by Beth Polouski. Three generations of woman enjoy a stroll through a tranquil Japanese garden in this enchanting quilted wall hanging. Create it using the appliqué method of your choice. If you plan to use a raw-edge technique, use the patterns as they are. If you plan to use a basted under edge technique, add ⅜ inch when cutting out each pattern (for this method the patterns are marked with a small "v" along edges which will not be turned under).

YOU WILL NEED
- Sun Showers pattern
- Fabrics
  - ¾ yard floral for Background, multi-hued
  - ¼ yard for Pathway, tan
  - Scraps for Bush 1, 2, & 3, green
  - Scrap for Water, blue
  - Scrap for Face A, B, and C; Arm A and B; Hand A and C, cream
  - Scrap for Hair A, B, and C, black
  - Printed scraps for Umbrellas A, B, and C; Body A, B, and C; Obi A and C; Sleeve A
- Borders
  - ¾ yard floral cut 3½" x 18" and 3½" x 25"
- Backing
  - ⅞ yard floral cut 29" x 25"
- Cotton batting cut 29" x 25"
- Appliqué supplies
- Machine quilting supplies

1 Photocopy the patterns from the enclosed pattern sheet twice. Tape one set together to create a full-sized placement guide. Use the other set for the actual templates. Prepare the templates and fabric according to your desired appliqué technique.

2 Cut the background fabric 24 x 19 inches.

3 Using the appliqué technique of your choice, attach the appliqué pieces in this order:

Attach the path. Then attach Bush 1, Bush 2, and Bush 3. Attach water.

Attach Umbrella B, Face B, Body B, Hair B, and Arm B.

Attach Umbrella A, Face A, Hair A, Body A, Obi A, Arm A, Hand A, and Sleeve A.

Attach Umbrella C, Face C, Hair C, Body C, Obi C, and Hand C.

4 Add umbrella handles using embroidery or permanent fabric markers.

5 Trim the block to 17½ x 21½ inches. Sew the smaller border strip to the left side, and then sew on the top border strip.

6 Layer backing, batting, and top. Baste using your preferred method.

7 Machine quilt in a free-flowing design.

8 Bind.

PROJECT 4
Silk Cover-up

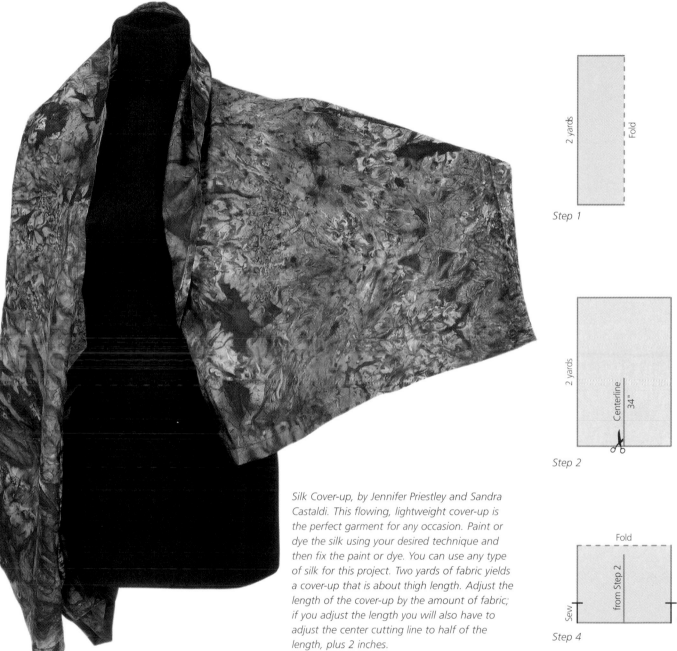

Silk Cover-up, by Jennifer Priestley and Sandra Castaldi. This flowing, lightweight cover-up is the perfect garment for any occasion. Paint or dye the silk using your desired technique and then fix the paint or dye. You can use any type of silk for this project. Two yards of fabric yields a cover-up that is about thigh length. Adjust the length of the cover-up by the amount of fabric; if you adjust the length you will also have to adjust the center cutting line to half of the length, plus 2 inches.

1 Fold the fabric in half, salvage to salvage, to find the center (it should now equal 2 yards by 22 inches). Finger-press the centerline.

2 Open the fabric up. Measure 34 inches from the bottom raw edge up the centerline. Cut up the centerline to the 34-inch measured mark.

3 Create a narrow rolled hem around the entire perimeter and up and down both sides of the center cut line.

4 Fold the silk in half lengthwise, inside out (so it is 1 yard by 44 inches). Starting at the bottom raw edge and stopping 10 inches from the fold for the armhole, sew the side seams using a ⅝-inch seam allowance.

YOU WILL NEED
- 2 yards x 44" wide silk
- Scissors
- Sewing machine and matching thread

Step 1

Step 2

Step 4

Recommended Reading

Barber, Barbara. *Broderie Perse: The Elegant Quilt*. Paducah, KY: American Quilter's Society. 1997.

Boughton, Kate. *Textile Dyeing: The Step-by-step Guide and Showcase*. Rockport, MA: Rockport Publications. 1995.

Doak, Carol. *Easy Reversible Vests*. Woodinville, WA: Martingale & Co. 1995.

Lawler, Mickey. *Skydyes: A Visual Guide to Fabric Painting*. Concord, CA: C&T Publishing. 1999.

Moller, Elfriede. *Shibori: The Art of Fabric Tying, Folding, Pleating and Dyeing*. Petaluma, CA: Search Press. 1999.

Mori, Joyce and Cynthia Myerberg. *Dye It! Paint It! Quilt It!*. Iola, WI: Krause Publications. 1996. (Both authors are national teachers; contact Joyce Mori at jmori@labyrinth.net and Cynthia Myerberg at Myerberg@worldnet.att.net.)

Noble, Elin. *Dyes & Paints: A Hands-On Guide to Coloring Fabric*. Bothell, WA: Fiber Studio Press. 1998.

Shay, Joan. *Petal Play the Traditional Way*. Paducah, KY: American Quilter's Society. 2001.

Smith, Louisa. *Strips 'n Curves*. Concord, CA: C&T Publishing. 2001.

True, Peggy. *True Style Pieced Jackets with Distinctive Appliqué*. Woodinville, WA: TPP. 1997. (Only available from the author; 511 Mt. Davidson Ct., Clayton, CA 94517; 925-672-4358; TruWay@aol.com)

Wells, Kate. *Fabric Dyeing & Printing*. Loveland, CO: Interweave Press. 1997.

Young, Blanche and Darlene Young. *Tradition with a Twist*. Concord, CA: C&T Publishing. 1996.

Close-up of Aquarium #1: Fish Tails, by Caryl Bryer Fallert, page 83.

Resources

The Authors

Cindy Walter
c/o Krause Publications
700 E. State Street
Iola, WI 54990-0001
snippetsensation@aol.com
www.cindywalter.com
Internationally known speaker, teacher, quilt designer, and commercial fabric designer. Author of *Snippet Sensations*, *More Snippet Sensations*, *Fine Hand Quilting*, and *Attic Windows*.

Jennifer Priestley
Fabrics To Dye For
Two River Road
Pawcatuck, CT 06379
888-322-1319
Jennifer@FabricsToDyeFor.com
www.FabricsToDyeFor.com
Fabric painter, teacher, and commercial fabric designer. Owner of Fabrics To Dye For.

Sources and Suppliers

Alaska Dyeworks
322 Ogden St.
P.O. Box 697
Village of Oxford, NE 68967-0697
308-824-3540
Wholesale and retail hand-dyed cotton.

Caryl Bryer Fallert
Bryerpatch Studio
P.O. Box 945
Oswego, IL 60543
www.bryerpatch.com
Award-winning quilt designer and international speaker.

Laura Cater Woods
315 Burlington Ave.
Billings, MT 59101
Fiber artist and instructor.

Dharma Trading Company
P.O. Box 150916
San Rafael, CA 94915
800-542-5227
www.dharmatrading.com
Mail order retail and wholesale dye, paint, and a large inventory of pre-made PFD clothing.

Fabrics To Dye For
Two River Road
Pawcatuck, CT 06379
888-322-1319
www.FabricsToDyeFor.com
Mail order retail and wholesale. Carries all supplies mentioned in this book, including patterns, dyes, paints, kits, PFD cotton, steamers, and books.

Giant Steps Therapeutic Equestrian Center, Inc.
595 Deer Creek Ln.
Petaluma, CA 94952-4770
www.giantstepsriding.org
Non-profit therapeutic equestrian center.

Jacquard Products
P.O. Box 425
Healdsburg, CA 95448
800-442-0455
www.jacquardproducts.com
Mail order retail and wholesale of dyes, paints, and a large array of silk and other fabrics.

Java House Quilts
2412 Majano Pl.
Carlsbad, CA 92009
Quilt patterns.

Melody Johnson Art Quilts
664 W. Main St.
Cary, IL 60013
www.artfabrik.com
Retail hand-dyed fabrics.

Mickey Lawler
Skydyes
P.O. Box 370116
West Hartford, CT 06137-0116
www.skydyes.com
Retail hand-painted fabrics.

Lorraine Torrence Designs
2112 S. Spokane St.
Seattle, WA 98144
800-369-4974
www.lorrainetorrence.com
Pattern designer and international speaker/teacher.

Lunn Fabrics
357 Santa Fe Dr.
Denver, CO 80223
303-623-2710
Retail hand-dyed and -painted fabrics.

Oriental Silks Co.
8377 Beverly Blvd.
Los Angeles, CA 90048
Wholesale and retail silk.

Petal Play
102 Courtney Rd.
Harwich, MA 02645
508-430-0347
www.PetalPlay.com
Appliqué quilt patterns.

PRO Chemical & Dye, Inc.
P.O. Box 14
Somerset, MA 02726
508-676-3838
or 800-2-buy-dye
www.prochemical.com
Mail order catalog, retail and wholesale.

Rupert, Gibbon & Spider, Inc.
Makers of Jacquard products
P.O. Box 425
Healdsburg, CA 95448
800-442-0455
www.jacquardproducts.com
Mail order retail and wholesale of dyes, paints, and large array of silk.

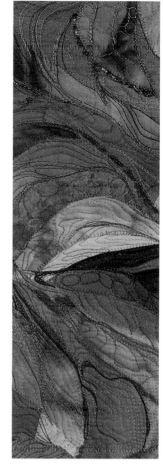

Close-up of Echo/Fragment #4, by Laura Cater-Woods, page 73.

Cindy and Jennifer have designed a small collection of paints for you to experiment with.

Close-up of one quilt from Melody Johnson's Chamber Series. The series includes five works, completed in February 2000. For more information, see page 64.

Linda S. Schmidt
Short Attention Span Quilting
7695 Sunwood Dr.
Dublin, CA 94568
925-829-4329
http://members.home.net/shortattn
shortattn@home.com
Custom quilt and garment designer, international speaker/teacher.

Shades Textiles
585 Cobb Parkway S, Nunn Complex "O"
Marietta, GA 30060-9302
770-919-9824
www.shadestextiles.com
Retail and wholesale hand-dyed cotton.

Testfabrics, Inc.
P.O. Box 26
W. Pittstown, PA 18643
717-603-0432
Mail order PFD fabric.

Thai Silks
252 State St.
Los Altos, CA 94022
800-722-7455
Mail order silk.

Tsukineko, Inc.
15411 NE 95th St.
Redmond, WA 98052
425-883-7733
www.tsukineko.com
Retail and wholesale All-Purpose Ink for fabric.

The Warm Company
954 Union St.
Seattle, WA 98122
800-234-Warm
www.warmcompany.com
Makers of quilted muslin and Warm n' Natural batting.

Index